Eating Economically is Just Plain <u>Smart</u>

How We Feed Our Family of 7 For Less Than $50 Per Week

Mary Jane & Jeff Cardarelle-Hermans

Published by
Mary Jane and Jeff Cardarelle-Hermans
410 W. Montclaire Avenue
Glendale, WI 53217

Printed in the United States of America

Library of Congress Catalog Card Number: 97-92807

ISBN: 0-9661400-0-1

Cover design and illustration by Lightbourne Images,
Copyright © 1998

Editorial Consultant: Nancy Stohs

CONTENTS

INTRODUCTION

People are amazed when they find out how little money we spend each week to feed our family of seven. The conversation usually begins when they find out that we have five children and they remark that it must be expensive to feed all those kids. When we tell them that we spend only about $50 a week, they look confused. They are usually a family of four that spends more than $150 a week. We hope this book will help you see how easy it is to lower the amount you spend each week on groceries. The following pages describe our family and how we were able to lower our grocery bill to less than $50 a week.

We adopted our five children on December 29th, 1993 in Madison, Wisconsin. We know what you're thinking-wow, what a big adjustment-but really it wasn't. In September of 1989, two of our boys moved in with us as foster children. Our other three children were placed in two other foster homes (they are all biological siblings). We were living in an apartment at the time and had room for only two children.

On many weekends all of our children would gather at our home to visit each other. We got to know all five of them very well. In July of 1990, we bought our first home in Madison, and in October our other two boys moved in with us.

Well, we now had four little boys to feed, and that is when we started concerning ourselves with the amount of money we were spending each week on groceries.

We now paid attention to the fact that a box of cornflakes was half the price of a box of pre-sweetened cereal. Oatmeal in a 42-ounce canister made a lot more oatmeal than 12 individual packages of instant oatmeal and for a lot less money. Ground turkey was less costly than ground beef. A 10-pound bag of potatoes was a better buy than frozen french fries or hash browns. Frozen concentrated orange juice was less expensive than buying orange juice in a refrigerated carton. Going out to eat with four little boys wasn't much fun, so we cut way back on that, too.

Cooking from scratch was almost always less expensive than buying prepackaged dinners, so we started avoiding many convenience foods. We borrowed cookbooks from the library and started creating our own low-cost meals.

We chose not to give the kids Kool-Aid because water was just as refreshing. A fruit roll-up was more expensive than the fruit itself, so why buy it? When it was time to celebrate the kids' birthdays, we decided to make their cakes from scratch. Making homemade cupcakes was cheaper than buying Twinkies.

At first, we used coupons quite a bit, thinking that they were saving us a great deal of money. But as time passed, we noticed we were using fewer and fewer because the coupons were usually for overpriced prepackaged food that we had stopped buying. Coupons can fool you into thinking you're saving money when in reality you're not because the foods are priced so high to begin with. We buy house-brand or store-brand items frequently over name-brand items. Most often house-brands are of equal quality, even if the taste is slightly different.

We also started checking the unit pricing so that we could get the best deals per ounce. Larger packages are usually, but not always, a better deal.

As time passed and the boys grew, our grocery bill did not go up. If anything, it kept going down as we learned more ways to save. Then sometime in early 1993, we found out that our kids had been released for adoption. Our daughter was still with her original foster family at that time, but that family decided not to adopt her. So in September of 1993, she moved in with us.

At that point, it was time to move into a bigger house and on December 22nd, 1993, we did just that. We moved into our current 4-bedroom home in Glendale, Wisconsin. One week later, we adopted our five children.

Now that we were living in a new community, we had to find new places to shop. We did some comparison shopping so that we would know which stores provided the best buys. Though we won't go way out of our way to save a nickel on an item, we do shop at a combination of stores. This way we have greater buying power. We mainly grocery shop at three different places. We shop at a health food store for items we can't find at a regular grocery store or that are a better buy. This store is about four miles from our house, and we shop there about once a month.

We shop at a discount supermarket chain once a week that is about eight miles from our house. This is where we buy many of our groceries. At this store, you won't find many name-brand items, and you have to pay with cash or food stamps. The store does not accept checks, credit cards or coupons. You have to bring your own bags or pay for theirs, and you have to bag your own groceries. They do not have the variety that other grocery stores have, and you have to be patient enough to stand in line, but the prices at this place are very low. To give you an idea of just how low, here is a list of some of the things we buy there and the prices we pay.

Chunk Tuna	6-oz. can	.49
Corn Oil	48 fl. oz.	1.79
Corn Flakes	18-oz. box	.89
Cream of Mushroom Soup	10¾-oz. can	.39
Egg Noodles	12-oz. bag	.49
Flour	5-lb. bag	.79
Fresh Carrots	2-lb. bag	.69
Frozen Vegetables	16-oz. bag	.79
Granulated Sugar	5-lb bag	1.89
Grape Jelly	32-oz. jar	.99
Ground Turkey-frozen	1 lb.	.69
Ketchup	28-oz. bottle	.69
Kidney Beans	15-oz. can	.29
Mayonnaise	32-oz. jar	1.29
Orange & Apple Juice (frozen concentrate)	12-oz. can	.69
Pancake Syrup	24 fl. oz.	.79
Peanut Butter	18-oz. jar	1.19
Quick Oats	42-oz.	1.29
Raisins	15-oz. box	.99
Refried Beans	16-oz. can	.39
Rice	32-oz. bag	.69

Saltine Crackers	16-oz. box	.59
Soda	12-pack	1.79
Spaghetti Sauce	30-oz. jar	1.29
Spaghetti Noodles	32-oz. box	.89
Tomato Paste	6-oz. can	.29
Tomato Soup	10¾-oz. can	.39
Tomato Sauce	8-oz. can	.19
Whole-Peeled Tomatoes	14.5-oz. can	.39
(10) - Tortilla Shells	17.5-oz.	.79

These were the prices for the last quarter of 1997, right before our book went into print. You can see that these are good prices.

We shop at a regular grocery store about once every two weeks. This is about six miles from our house and on the way to the discount supermarket chain. Here we buy items that the discount chain doesn't carry (such as popcorn and fresh sprouts). Sometimes this store has sales that make some foods less expensive than at the discount chain. It may sound as though we do a lot of running around, but really we don't. It takes us about two hours from the time we leave our house to when we return home, one day per week, to get all of our shopping done.

Our kids now range in age from 8 to 17 and are growing every day. Two of our sons clearly eat more than both of us (put together, it sometimes seems). Our daughter and one of our sons eat about the same as mom, and our other son eats about as much as dad.

Yet we always have an abundance of food.

Yes, we can afford to spend more money on groceries, but why would we want to? Eating economically is just plain smart.

What exactly do we buy each week? We don't buy each item every week, but the following is a list of everything we keep in the pantry, refrigerator and freezer.

Baking Supplies:
Baking powder, baking soda, salt, unsweetened cocoa powder, dry yeast, eggs, egg substitute and vinegar.

We buy yeast in bulk at the health food store because it is a lot less expensive per pound than at a regular grocery store.

We buy Ener-G egg Replacer at the health food store. We use it in place of eggs in almost all of our baking recipes (although we don't indicate that in the recipes). It ends up being less expensive than using eggs. It also contains no fat or cholesterol and is lower in calories than eggs. (It does not work in the pumpkin pie recipe.)

Breads:
Whole wheat loaves, bagels, saltines, flour tortilla shells, all-purpose crackers, hamburger buns.

We make a lot of our own breads in addition to buying those just indicated.

Cheese:
Shredded mozzarella cheese, shredded and block cheddar cheese, cream cheese, sour cream.

We buy sour cream only occasionally.

We use cream cheese only on bagels.

Cereal:
Cornflakes, Malt-o-Meal.

We buy a house/store brand box of cornflakes, and this is usually the only cold cereal we eat. Occasionally we buy bran flakes, too.

Condiments:
Ketchup, mayonnaise, mustard, strawberry preserves, grape jelly.

Fats:
100% real butter, corn oil.

Fruits:
Apples, bananas, raisins, pears, grapefruit, oranges, watermelon, etc.

We try to buy seasonal fruit because it usually is the lowest priced.

We do not buy any canned fruit.

Fish:
Canned tuna (water-packed)

Grains:
All-purpose flour, whole-wheat flour, oatmeal, yellow cornmeal, white rice, brown rice, popcorn.

We use brown rice instead of white rice in many of our recipes even though it is more expensive. This is because natural brown rice is naturally rich in nutrients and fiber. Brown rice does, however, take a little longer to prepare.

We use whole-wheat flour in many of our recipes even though whole-wheat flour costs more than white flour. This is because whole-wheat flour is less processed and better for you; it contains more nutrients and dietary fiber.

We have our own popcorn popper (West Bend Stir Crazy corn popper) and pop popcorn frequently for snacks. We would never waste money on microwave popcorn or on already-popped corn.

Juices:
Orange and apple.

We buy these in the 12-ounce frozen concentrated juice form(unsweetened), which is less expensive than cartons of juice sold in the refrigerator section of the store.

Legumes:
Peanut butter, canned kidney beans, canned garbanzo beans, refried beans, tofu, dried white beans.

We buy both crunchy and creamy peanut butter for variety.

We buy 15-ounce cans of kidney beans. You can also buy dry kidney beans and cook them yourself. Two cups cooked will equal approximately 1 can of kidney beans in any of our recipes.

We buy 16-ounce cans of refried beans.

Meat:
Frozen ground turkey, frozen chicken quarters.

Meat Substitute:
Texturized soy protein granules.

We buy texturized soy protein, which is often called TSP or TVP at the health food store, in bulk. It comes dry and needs to be rehydrated before using it. When rehydrated, it has a texture similar to ground beef or ground turkey. We pour 7/8 cup of boiling water over 1 cup of TSP, stir and let it sit about 10 minutes. We then use it as we would a pound of cooked ground meat.

TSP is less expensive than ground meat and is lower in fat and calories. It can be used in many of our recipes and is great if you are a vegetarian.

Milk:
Dry milk, gallons of 2% or skim milk.

We sometimes use nonfat dry milk in recipes that call for milk because generally it is less expensive than milk in gallon cartons. In recipes, the taste difference cannot be detected. It also makes good hot cocoa.

Non-nutritious Beverages:
Ground coffee, carbonated soda.

Our family does not drink coffee, but we do have it on hand for when we have guests over who drink it.

There are no nutritional benefits in soda, and this should be kept in mind when you decide how often you are going to buy it.

Pastas:
Spaghetti, elbow macaroni, egg noodles, lasagna.

Seasonings and Flavorings:

Soy sauce, pure vanilla extract, ground cinnamon, pepper, cumin, vegetable-flavored bouillon granules, dried parsley, dried basil, dried thyme, garlic powder, paprika, bay leaves, dried rosemary, celery salt, dried oregano, dry mustard, chili powder, onion powder, turmeric.

You can add your own favorites to this list.

Sweeteners:

Granulated sugar, brown sugar, powdered sugar.

Soups, Sauces, Syrups:

Condensed tomato soup and cream of mushroom soup, spaghetti sauce, pancake syrup.

Even though we include a spaghetti sauce recipe in this book, we rarely make it. We usually just buy spaghetti sauce in a jar or can at the grocery store. It is not much more expensive.

We have included a cream of onion soup recipe to be used instead of cream of mushroom soup in our recipes. This will be less expensive than buying cans of cream of mushroom soup, but we still like to have the cans in the pantry for when we are not in the mood to make the cream of onion soup.

Vegetables:

Cabbage, onions, celery, carrots, potatoes, tomato sauce, tomato paste, whole peeled tomatoes, frozen spinach, frozen corn, frozen peas, frozen broccoli, frozen green beans, zucchini, canned pumpkin, cucumber, lettuce, sprouts, garlic, green pepper, rhubarb.

We buy all of our vegetables either fresh or frozen except for the canned pumpkin, tomato sauce, tomato paste and whole peeled tomatoes.

We have rhubarb only because we have a patch in our back yard.

We have a small food garden in which we grow green beans, tomatoes, carrots, green peppers and beets.

This includes everything we buy at the grocery store. Once in a while we will stray from this list, but not usually. When items go on sale, we stock up so that we get them for the lowest price.

In the following chapters, we talk about the different meals of the day and the desserts we feed our family. It will give you an idea of specifically what we are eating at our house and when we are eating it. You will also find most of the recipes we use to feed our bunch. We hope you enjoy these recipes and good luck on saving more money on your future grocery bills.

BREAKFAST

Breakfast at our house does not usually begin with a bowl of cereal. Most breakfast cereals are overpriced and over-processed, filled with synthetic coloring and flavorings, tons of sugar and added preservatives.

If you are one of the people making breakfast cereal choices based on marketing hype, fancy packaging and coupons, ask yourself this: is more money being spent on the package than on the product itself? We buy cornflakes, occasionally bran flakes and if our family eats cold cereal once a week, that's about it.

Let's listen to the surgeon general's recommendations to increase the intake of fruits, vegetables and whole grains. Why not start the day off with a piece of seasonal fresh fruit and a bowl of oatmeal or pancakes made with whole-wheat flour? Why not feed your family a piece of fruit along with some whole-wheat toast or a muffin on some days?

You say you don't have time to make breakfast? Putting a piece of bread in the toaster and grabbing a piece of fruit out of the refrigerator doesn't take very long. Save the pancakes or fried potatoes for the weekend when you have more time. Make muffins on the weekend for the next week. Quick-cooking oatmeal doesn't take very long. Neither do scrambled eggs. Make the time. Cooking nutritious food for your family is an act of great love. You are the guardian of your children/families' health and you have a responsibility and obligation to supply them with foods that will best promote their health and vitality. So our suggestion is to start the day off by skipping the overpriced colored cereal and other over-processed convenience breakfast foods and eating a more nutritious, low-cost breakfast instead.

MUFFINS

2 cups flour
1 Tablespoon baking powder
½ teaspoon salt
1/3 cup sugar
¼ cup oil
1 cup milk
2 eggs
½ cup raisins (optional)

1. Preheat oven to 400 degrees.
2. In large mixing bowl, combine flour, baking powder, salt, and sugar. Mix briefly with a fork.
3. Add oil, milk and eggs to dry ingredients. Stir with a fork until completely mixed, using a rubber spatula to scrape sides of bowl if necessary. When completely mixed, add raisins and stir in.
4. Lightly grease 12 muffin cups in muffin pan with butter. Divide batter evenly among muffin cups.
5. Bake in preheated oven for 15 to 20 minutes or until muffins are light to medium brown and a toothpick inserted into center of muffins comes out clean.
6. Let muffins cool in pan briefly on top of stove or on wire rack. Muffins should come out easily, but you might need to run a knife around the edge of each cup.

This recipe makes 12 muffins.

Substitute one cup of orange juice for the cup of milk in this recipe to make "ORANGE MUFFINS."

To make **"JELLY FILLED MUFFINS,"** *add only half the amount of batter in the muffin cups as you normally would. Then drop a heaping teaspoon of jelly on top. Then add the other half of the batter and bake as usual.*

CRUMB TOPPING FOR MUFFINS

½ cup sugar
½ cup flour
¼ cup butter

1. Place sugar and flour in medium mixing bowl. Mix with a fork until well combined.
2. Add butter. Mix with a fork or pastry cutter until completely combined and evenly mixed.
3. Add 1 teaspoon of crumb topping to the top of any unbaked muffins. Bake muffins as usual.

OATMEAL CINNAMON MUFFINS

1 + 1/3 cups flour
¾ cup quick-cooking rolled oats
1/3 cup packed brown sugar
2 teaspoons baking powder
¼ teaspoon salt
¼ teaspoon ground cinnamon
¼ cup oil
¾ cup milk
1 egg
½ cup raisins (optional)

1. Preheat oven to 400 degrees.
2. In large mixing bowl combine flour, rolled oats, brown sugar, baking powder, salt and cinnamon. Mix briefly with a fork to combine dry ingredients.
3. Add oil, milk and egg. Mix wet ingredients together with dry ingredients with your fork. When completely mixed, add raisins and stir in.
4. Lightly grease 12 muffin cups in muffin pan with butter. Divide batter evenly among muffin cups.
5. Bake in preheated oven 15 to 20 minutes or until muffins are golden and a toothpick inserted into center of muffins comes out clean.
6. Let muffins cool in pan briefly on top of stove or on wire rack. Muffins should come out easily, but you might need to run a knife around the edge of each cup.

This recipe makes 12 muffins.

APPLE MUFFINS

1 cup chopped apples
2 cups flour
1 Tablespoon baking powder
¼ teaspoon salt
¼ teaspoon ground cinnamon
1/3 cup packed brown sugar
¼ cup oil
¾ cup milk
2 eggs

1. Preheat oven to 400 degrees.
2. Peel and cut enough small apple pieces to yield one cup. Set apple pieces aside.
3. In large mixing bowl combine flour, baking powder, salt, cinnamon and brown sugar. Mix briefly with a fork to combine dry ingredients.
4. Add oil, milk and eggs to dry ingredients. Stir with a fork until completely mixed, using a rubber spatula to scrape sides of bowl if necessary. When completely mixed, add apple pieces and stir in.
5. Lightly grease 12 muffin cups in muffin pan with butter. Divide batter evenly among muffin cups.
6. Bake in preheated oven for 15 to 20 minutes or until muffins are light to medium brown and a toothpick inserted into center of muffins comes out clean.
7. Let muffins cool in pan briefly on top of stove or on wire rack. Muffins should come out easily, but you might need to run a knife around the edge of each cup.

This recipe makes 12 muffins.

BANANA MUFFINS

2 bananas
2 cups flour
1/3 cup sugar
1 Tablespoon baking powder
½ teaspoon salt
½ cup milk
¼ cup oil
1 egg

1. Preheat oven to 400 degrees.
2. Peel and put bananas in large mixing bowl. Mash bananas with a fork until they are very mushy.
3. Add flour, sugar, baking powder, salt, milk, oil and egg. Mix with electric mixer until thoroughly combined, scraping sides of bowl with rubber spatula as necessary.
4. Lightly grease 12 muffin cups with butter. Divide batter evenly among muffin cups.
5. Bake in preheated oven approximately 20 minutes or until muffins are light brown and a toothpick inserted into center of muffins comes out clean.
6. Let muffins cool in pan briefly on top of stove or on wire rack. Muffins should come out easily, but you might need to run a knife around the edge of each cup.

This recipe makes 12 muffins.

Substitute 1 cup of solid pack pumpkin and ¼ of a teaspoon of cinnamon for the bananas to make **"PUMPKIN MUFFINS."** *To make* **"ZUCCHINI MUFFINS,"** *substitute 1 cup grated zucchini for the bananas.*

OATMEAL

1 cup water
½ cup quick-cooking rolled oats

1. Bring water to boil in small saucepan over high heat.
2. Add rolled oats and stir. Reduce heat to low and simmer 1 to 2 minutes, stirring occasionally. Turn off heat and let oatmeal sit a little while until it gets thick.
3. Pour oatmeal into a bowl and serve it with brown sugar and milk, if desired .

This recipe makes one serving.

To make **"APPLE/CINNAMON OATMEAL,"** *add 1/8 teaspoon cinnamon, 1 Tablespoon raisins and ½ cup chopped apples when you add the oatmeal to the boiling water.*

HOT CORNMEAL

1 cup yellow cornmeal
5 cups water (divided)
1 teaspoon salt (optional)

1. Place cornmeal in medium mixing bowl. Add 1 cup water. Mix with a fork until combined. Let mixture sit 5 minutes.
2. Pour remaining 4 cups water in large saucepan. Add salt. Over high heat, bring water and salt to a boil.
3. When water is boiling rapidly, add cornmeal mixture. Stir mixture continually with whisk until mixture is thick and free of lumps. Cover saucepan.
4. Reduce heat to low and simmer approximately 10 to 15 minutes, stirring occasionally. Be careful when you remove the lid because cornmeal boils in "bursts" that can fly up and burn your hand.
5. When cornmeal is done, divide it between 4 bowls and serve with brown sugar and milk.

This recipe makes 4 servings.

FRIED POTATOES

10 cups diced or cubed potatoes
½ cup chopped onion (optional)
3 Tablespoons oil
½ teaspoon salt
1/8 teaspoon pepper

1. Wash and cut enough potatoes to yield 10 cups of cubed potatoes. You can leave the peeling on if you wish.
2. Place potatoes in an electric frying pan. Add onions, if desired. Drizzle oil over potatoes. Add salt and pepper.
3. Turn the electric frying pan to 350 degrees. Mix potatoes, oil, salt and pepper with a metal or plastic spatula.
4. Cook potatoes approximately 20 minutes. Stir potatoes every few minutes, scraping bottom of frying pan and bringing bottom potatoes to the top so they are evenly cooked. When potatoes are done, serve plain or with ketchup.

This recipe makes about 7½ cups of
cooked potatoes, about 6 to 8 servings.

PANCAKES/WAFFLES

2 cups flour
2 teaspoons baking powder
¼ teaspoon salt
2 eggs
2 cups milk
4 Tablespoons oil
2 teaspoons vanilla extract

1. Preheat a lightly greased griddle or electric frying pan to 350 degrees. Preheat a waffle maker if making waffles.
2. In large mixing bowl, combine flour, baking powder and salt, mixing with a fork until well combined.
3. Add eggs, milk, oil and vanilla. Mix batter with electric mixer or whisk until well combined. Scrape sides of bowl with rubber spatula if necessary.
4. For each pancake, pour ¼ cup batter onto the hot, lightly greased griddle or electric frying pan. Cook until bottom half is browned, then flip pancake with firm spatula and brown other side. If making waffles, follow the waffle maker instruction manual to determine how much batter to pour into the waffle maker and when the waffles are done.

Serve with butter and syrup. This recipe makes approximately 16 four-inch pancakes or 20 four-inch square waffles.

To make **"WHOLE-WHEAT PANCAKES,"** *substitute 1 cup of whole-wheat flour for 1 cup of flour in this recipe.*

If the batter seems a little too runny, add a little more flour. If the batter seems a little too thick, add a little more milk.

FRENCH TOAST

2 eggs
1 cup milk
12 slices bread

1. Preheat a lightly greased griddle or electric frying pan to 350 degrees.
2. Break 2 eggs into large mixing bowl. Add milk. Beat mixture together with whisk or fork until well combined.
3. Dip slices of bread into mixture, coating each side. Fry on each side until light to medium brown.

Serve with butter and syrup.
This recipe makes approximately 4 servings.

SCRAMBLED EGGS

12 eggs
¾ cup milk
½ teaspoon salt
1/8 teaspoon pepper
1 Tablespoon butter

1. Break eggs into large mixing bowl. Add milk, salt and pepper.
2. Mix these ingredients together with whisk or electric mixer on low speed until well combined.
3. Preheat electric frying pan to 350 degrees.
4. Add butter and let it melt, spreading melted butter evenly across bottom of pan.
5. Add egg mixture. Cook eggs until fluffy and lightly browned. You will need to stir these with a hard spatula often to avoid burning bottom of eggs and uneven cooking.

This recipe makes approximately 6 servings.

<u>Recipe Variation:</u>

Add ½ cup chopped onion when you add the butter and saute until tender, then go on to step 5.

Add ½ cup grated cheddar cheese after eggs are done; cover and let cheese melt.

LUNCH

Our family's lunches do <u>not</u> include the school hot lunch program or restaurant lunches. If you are letting your kids eat hot lunch or are dining out over your lunch hour, you are spending money unnecessarily, money that could be put to good use somewhere else.

A nutritious, healthful, brown bag lunch can cost well under $1. At our children's schools, the hot lunch program costs $1.60 per day at the elementary school, $1.65 at the middle school and $1.75 at the high school. We can save well over $1 per day per child just by taking the time to pack them a cold lunch. This is a significant amount considering we have five children.

By packing them a cold lunch, we save over $5 per day. The kids go to school approximately 180 days per year, so we save well over $900 per year just by packing them a cold lunch instead of allowing them to take hot lunch.

The savings is even greater when you avoid restaurants during your lunch hour. Let's say you spend on the average $4.50 per day dining out for lunch, and let's say you could pack a cold lunch for $.50. By packing a cold lunch you can save $4 per day. That's $20 per week. If you work 50 weeks in a year, you could save yourself $1,000 just by brown bagging it. If you work close to your home, why not go home during your lunch hour? When our family eats lunch at home, we seem to just start pulling things out of the refrigerator. We might have leftovers from previous dinners. Often we will have soup, salad and sandwiches.

The following is a list of things we typically put in a brown bag lunch:
Fresh fruit: peeled, sliced or whole
Fresh vegetables: cut-up carrots, celery, broccoli, etc.
Sandwiches: a variety made on homemade bread, store bought-bread or bagels.
Snacks: popcorn, muffins, homemade cookies or cupcakes.
Plastic reusable beverage containers with juice or water inside, or sometimes a soda.

We do not rely on processed or convenience food. Brightly colored, packaged candy, cookies and chips are rarely allowed. These individually packaged fun foods have the highest mark-up. Again, don't make food choices based on marketing hype, fancy packaging or coupons. If your children complain, tell them that you are saving the Earth by buying foods with less packaging (it's true). Our suggestion is to make your own snacks. They are a lot less expensive. Substitute fruit and vegetables for sugary snacks and feed them popcorn instead of buying potato chips. Make sure your family's lunches are packed with love, not additives.

The following recipes will give you an idea of what we eat for lunch. This is a small section because there is no recipe for many of the things we eat for lunch, including peanut butter and jelly sandwiches, popcorn, cut-up vegetables and fruit. Other regulars in our family's lunches are found in different sections of this book. For example, muffin recipes are found in the breakfast section; cookie recipes in the dessert section and a whole-wheat bread recipe in the bread section. Soups and salads are found in the soups and salads section.

HARD-BOILED EGGS

8 eggs

1. Put eggs in medium saucepan. Pour in enough water to cover.
2. Bring water to a boil over high heat and boil eggs 10 minutes.
3. Remove eggs from heat and let sit in the water an additional 10 minutes.
4. Drain eggs. Rinse under cold water and then peel.

Makes 8 eggs.

EGG SALAD SANDWICH FILLING

4 hard-boiled eggs
3 Tablespoons mayonnaise
2 teaspoons prepared mustard
¼ cup chopped celery
Lettuce, sprouts, sliced cucumber (optional)

1. Peel hard-boiled eggs and place in a medium mixing bowl.
2. Add mayonnaise, mustard and celery.
3. Mix with a fork or a pastry cutter mashing eggs as you mix.
4. Spread between slices of bread. Add lettuce, sprouts, etc., as desired.

This will make enough for approximately 4 sandwiches.

TOFU
SANDWICH SPREAD

8 ounces firm tofu
2 Tablespoons chopped celery
1 Tablespoon chopped onion
½ teaspoon ground turmeric
½ teaspoon ground cumin
½ teaspoon salt
2 to 3 Tablespoons mayonnaise
Lettuce, sprouts (optional)

1. Place tofu in medium mixing bowl. Add celery, onion, turmeric, cumin, salt and mayonnaise.
2. Mash with pastry cutter or fork until it has a uniform consistency.
3. Spread between slices of bread. Add lettuce, sprouts, etc., as desired.

This recipe makes 1½ cups, enough
for 4 to 6 sandwiches.

TVP/KIDNEY BEAN SANDWICH SPREAD

1 cup TVP (texturized vegetable protein)
7/8 cup boiling water
1 Tablespoon oil
1 cup chopped onion
2 cloves garlic, minced
1 can (15-ounce) kidney beans, drained
¼ cup yellow mustard
½ teaspoon salt
½ teaspoon ground cumin
Lettuce, sprouts, sliced cucumbers (optional)

1. Pour TVP into medium mixing bowl. Boil water in medium saucepan on stove.
2. When water is boiling, pour it over TVP. Stir mixture with a fork and let it sit 10 minutes until all the water is absorbed.
3. Put 1 Tablespoon oil in a saucepan. Add onion and garlic. Saute onion and garlic over medium heat until onions are soft, approximately 5 minutes.
4. Put kidney beans, rehydrated TVP, sauteed onions and garlic, mustard, salt and cumin in a food processor. Blend until smooth.
5. Spread about ¼ cup of the sandwich spread between 2 slices of bread. Add lettuce, sprouts, sliced cucumbers, etc., as desired.

This recipe makes approximately 3 cups, enough
for approximately 12 sandwiches.

TUNA SALAD SANDWICH SPREAD

1 can (6-ounce) tuna, drained
¼ cup mayonnaise or salad dressing
1/8 cup chopped celery
Lettuce, sprouts (optional)

1. Place drained tuna in small mixing bowl. Break apart chunks of tuna with a fork.
2. Add mayonnaise and chopped celery. Mix together with a fork until well combined.
3. Spread between slices of bread. Add lettuce, sprouts, etc., as desired.

This recipe make approximately ¾ cup,
enough for approximately 3 sandwiches.

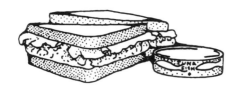

CHICKEN SALAD
SANDWICH SPREAD

1 cup chopped cooked chicken
¼ cup mayonnaise
1 to 2 teaspoons prepared mustard
¼ cup chopped celery
Lettuce, sprouts (optional)

1. Put chopped chicken in food processor and process until fine.
2. Transfer to medium mixing bowl. Add mayonnaise, mustard and chopped celery.
3. Mix until well combined.
4. Spread between slices of bread. Add lettuce, sprouts, etc., as desired.

This recipe makes 1 heaping cup, enough
for approximately 4 sandwiches.

GRILLED CHEESE SANDWICH

1 Tablespoon butter
2 slices bread
2 slices cheddar cheese

1. Spread thin coat of butter on one side of two slices of bread.
2. Put one slice of bread on griddle or electric frying pan with buttered side to the bottom. Add cheese.
3. Place other slice of bread on top with buttered side facing up.
4. Turn griddle or frying pan to 350 degrees.
5. Fry on each side until light to medium brown.

This recipe makes 1 sandwich.

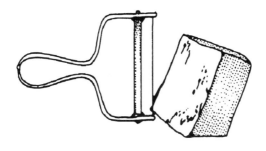

CHICKEN SALAD BURRITOS

1 cup leftover cooked chicken, cut up
1 cup chopped cucumber
1 cup shredded cheddar cheese
1 cup chopped lettuce
½ cup mayonnaise or salad dressing
5 soft flour tortillas

1. Place cut-up chicken in food processor. Process a few times until chicken is chopped into tiny pieces.
2. Transfer chicken to mixing bowl. Add cucumber, cheese, lettuce and mayonnaise. Mix until well combined.
3. Heat tortillas according to package directions.
4. Make burritos by placing ½ cup of the meat filling down the center of a warm tortilla.
5. Fold the two sides of the tortilla so that they overlap.

This recipe makes 5 burritos.

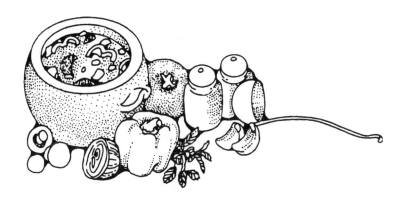

SOUPS & SALADS

This is one of our favorite sections because we eat a lot of vegetables. We make homemade salad dressing instead of buying it to save a bundle of money. These dressings are quick and easy to make. We also make homemade croutons. We eat the Main Course Salad as a meal for either lunch or dinner about once a week. We also make side salads to go along with dinners and sandwiches.

Homemade soups taste so much better and are less expensive than buying soups in cans. You can make coleslaw, potato salad or macaroni salad yourself and spend a lot less per pound than what you pay at the deli.

CHICKEN NOODLE SOUP

3 cups peeled and chopped carrots
1 cup chopped onion
1 cup chopped celery
2 cups leftover cooked chicken or turkey, cut up
10 cups water
1 Tablespoon vegetable-flavored bouillon granules
1 Tablespoon salt or to taste
1/8 teaspoon pepper
4 to 6 cups dry egg noodles

1. Place chopped carrots in large soup pot. Add chopped onion, celery and meat.
2. Add the water to soup pot, then add vegetable-flavored bouillon, salt and pepper.
3. Cover pot and bring soup to a boil over high heat.
4. When soup is boiling, reduce heat and simmer soup 30 minutes. Stir soup occasionally.
5. While soup is simmering, cook egg noodles according to package directions.
6. After soup has simmered 30 minutes, add the cooked noodles and stir in.
7. Bring soup to a boil and then simmer an additional 15 minutes.

This recipe makes approximately 14 to 16 one cup servings.

To make "CHICKEN POTATO SOUP," add 3 cups of peeled and chopped potatoes to the soup instead of the egg noodles. Add the potatoes in step 1 and skip steps 5 and 6.

To make **"CHICKEN AND RICE SOUP,"** *add 1 cup of uncooked rice to the soup instead of the egg noodles. Add the rice in step 1 and skip steps 5 and 6. If the soup is too thick at the end of the cooking time, add more water.*

POTATO SOUP

---

1 pound ground turkey
4 cups peeled and diced potatoes
1 cup chopped onion
3 cans (8-ounce) tomato sauce
4 cups water
2 teaspoons salt
¼ teaspoon pepper

1. Place ground turkey in frying pan and brown over medium heat, stirring until crumbly. Drain off any fat.
2. Transfer cooked meat to large soup pot. Add potatoes, onion, tomato sauce, water, salt and pepper. Stir soup until well combined.
3. Cover pot and bring soup to a boil over high heat.
4. When soup is boiling, reduce heat to low and simmer 1 hour, stirring occasionally. Soup is done when potatoes are tender.

This recipe makes approximately 10 cups.

CREAM OF BROCCOLI SOUP

1 bag (16-ounce) frozen chopped broccoli
½ cup chopped onion
3 cups milk
¼ cup flour
½ teaspoon salt
¼ teaspoon dried thyme
¼ teaspoon garlic powder
2 Tablespoon vegetable-flavored bouillon granules

1. Place broccoli in medium saucepan. Add onions. Add enough water to cover.
2. Cover pot and bring broccoli to a boil over high heat.
3. When broccoli is boiling, reduce heat to medium and continue boiling 10 minutes.
4. Meanwhile, pour milk into large soup pot. Add flour, salt, thyme, garlic powder and vegetable-flavored bouillon. Stir with a whisk until well combined.
5. Cook white sauce over medium-low heat, stirring with whisk until sauce becomes warm and thick.
6. When broccoli and onions are boiled, drain them.
7. Add broccoli and onions to white sauce. Mix until well combined.
8. Heat over low heat about 5 minutes, then serve immediately.

This recipe makes approximately 5 cups.

WHITE BEAN SOUP

2 cups navy beans (soak beans overnight)
10 cups water
2 cups diced carrots
1 cup diced celery
½ cup diced red or green pepper
1 cup diced onions
3 garlic cloves, minced
1 bay leaf
½ teaspoon dried rosemary
½ teaspoon dried thyme
1 Tablespoon salt
1/8 teaspoon pepper
1 Tablespoon vegetable-flavored bouillon granules (optional)

1. Drain beans and place in a soup pot with the 10 cups water. Add carrots, celery, pepper, onions, garlic, bay leaf, rosemary and thyme.
2. Cover pot and bring soup to a boil over high heat.
3. When soup is boiling, reduce heat to low and simmer 1 hour and 40 minutes.
4. After soup has simmered, add salt and pepper to taste. Add bouillon, if desired. Cook additional 30 to 40 minutes.

This recipe makes approximately 11 cups.

VEGETABLE CHOWDER

½ cup chopped onion
1 teaspoon minced garlic
1 cup chopped celery
1 cup peeled and chopped carrots
1 cup peeled and diced potatoes
2 cups frozen corn
4 cups water
4 teaspoons vegetable-flavored bouillon granules
1/8 teaspoon pepper
1/8 teaspoon paprika
2 Tablespoons butter
¼ cup flour
2 cups milk
1 Tablespoon prepared yellow mustard
2 cups grated cheddar cheese

1. Place onion, garlic, celery, carrots, potatoes, corn, water, vegetable-flavored bouillon, pepper and paprika in large soup pot.
2. Cover pot and bring soup to a boil over high heat. When soup is boiling, reduce heat to low and simmer 20 to 30 minutes or until potatoes are soft.
3. While soup is simmering, make cheese sauce.
4. Melt butter in medium saucepan over medium-low heat.
5. Add flour and stir with a whisk until mixed. Add milk and mustard. Cook sauce, stirring with a whisk until it thickens.
6. When sauce has thickened, add cheese. Stir until cheese melts. Remove sauce from burner.
7. After soup has simmered, add cheese sauce. Stir until completely mixed and heated through.

This recipe makes approximately 8 cups.

CREAM OF ONION SOUP (FOR CASSEROLES)

1 Tablespoon oil
½ cup chopped onion
1 teaspoon vegetable-flavored bouillon granules
½ teaspoon salt
1/8 teaspoon pepper (optional)
4 Tablespoons flour
1¼ cups milk

1. Place oil in small saucepan. Add onions. Saute over medium heat until onions are soft and slightly browned.
2. Add the vegetable-flavored bouillon, salt, pepper, flour and milk. Mix with a whisk until well combined.
3. Cook soup, stirring with a whisk continually until soup has thickened.

This recipe can be used in almost any recipe in the place of a can of cream of mushroom soup.

VEGETABLE SOUP WITH BASIL

1 cup chopped onion
1½ teaspoons minced garlic
1 cup diced celery
1 cup chopped cabbage
1 cup peeled and diced carrots
1 cup peeled and diced potatoes
1 cup green beans
2 cans (14.5-ounce) of whole peeled tomatoes, chopped
1 Tablespoon salt
2 Tablespoons soy sauce
1/8 teaspoon pepper
1 Tablespoon vegetable-flavored bouillon granules
½ Tablespoon dried parsley
1 teaspoon dried basil
9 cups water (divided)
1 cup dry elbow macaroni
1 can (16-ounce) red kidney beans

1. Place onion, garlic, celery, cabbage, carrots, potatoes, green beans and tomatoes in large soup pot.
2. Add salt, soy sauce, pepper, vegetable-flavored bouillon, parsley and basil. Add 5 cups of water.
3. Cover pot and bring mixture to a boil over high heat. When soup is boiling, reduce heat to low and simmer approximately 30 minutes.
4. While soup is simmering, cook elbow macaroni according to package directions.
5. When soup has simmered 30 minutes, add the cooked macaroni, kidney beans, and remaining 4 cups of water.

6. Increase heat to high and bring soup to a boil, then reduce heat to low and simmer another 15 minutes.

This recipe makes approximately 16 cups

<u>*Recipe Variation*</u>*:*
Instead of using elbow macaroni, you can use ½ cup uncooked rice. Add the uncooked rice in step 1 and skip step 4.

MAIN COURSE SALAD

---

3 cups leafy greens (lettuce, spinach, etc.) in any combination
1 cup cooked rice
½ cup cooked vegetables (corn, broccoli, peas, etc.)
½ cup chopped raw vegetables (sprouts, carrots, etc.)
¼ cup dressing of your choice

1. Tear enough leafy greens to yield 3 cups. Arrange on a large plate or in a bowl.
2. Add rice, cooked vegetables and raw vegetables.
3. Add salad dressing and mix until well combined.

This recipe makes 1 serving.

CREAMY GARLIC DRESSING

¼ cup vinegar
¼ cup mayonnaise
½ cup oil
2 teaspoons garlic powder
½ teaspoon salt
½ teaspoon dried thyme
1 teaspoon dried oregano

1. In medium mixing bowl, combine vinegar, mayonnaise, oil, garlic powder, salt, thyme and oregano.
2. Mix with a fork or a whisk until well combined.
3. Store dressing in covered container in refrigerator.

This recipe makes approximately 1 cup.

FRENCH DRESSING

¼ cup vinegar
½ cup ketchup
½ cup oil
¼ cup sugar
½ teaspoon salt
½ teaspoon paprika
1/8 teaspoon garlic powder

1. In medium mixing bowl, combine vinegar, ketchup, oil, sugar, salt, paprika and garlic powder.
2. Mix with a fork or a whisk until well combined.
3. Store dressing in covered container in refrigerator.

This recipe makes 1 and 1/3 cups.

ITALIAN VINAIGRETTE DRESSING

¼ cup vinegar
¾ cup oil
1 teaspoon garlic powder
½ teaspoon salt
¼ teaspoon pepper
½ Tablespoon parsley flakes
½ teaspoon dry mustard
¼ teaspoon dried oregano

1. In medium mixing bowl, combine vinegar, oil, garlic powder, salt, pepper, parsley, dry mustard and oregano.
2. Mix with a fork or a whisk until well combined.
3. Store dressing in covered container in refrigerator.

This recipe makes approximately 1 cup.

THOUSAND ISLAND DRESSING

¼ cup oil
¼ cup mayonnaise
2 Tablespoons vinegar
2 Tablespoons ketchup
2 teaspoons sugar
½ teaspoon salt
1 teaspoon parsley flakes
½ teaspoon paprika
1/8 teaspoon garlic powder

1. In medium mixing bowl, combine oil, mayonnaise, vinegar, ketchup, sugar, salt, parsley, paprika and garlic powder.
2. Mix with a fork or a whisk until well combined.
3. Store dressing in covered container in refrigerator.

This recipe makes approximately ¾ cup.

HOUSE DRESSING

¾ cup mayonnaise
½ cup milk
1 teaspoon vinegar
1 teaspoon parsley flakes
1 teaspoon garlic powder
½ teaspoon salt
1/8 teaspoon pepper

1. In medium mixing bowl, combine mayonnaise, milk, vinegar, parsley flakes, garlic powder, salt and pepper.
2. Mix with a fork or a whisk until well combined.
3. Store in covered container in refrigerator.

This recipe makes approximately 1¼ cups.

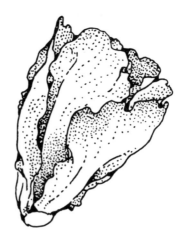

CROUTONS

2 Tablespoons oil
¼ teaspoon garlic powder
¼ teaspoon celery salt
¼ teaspoon dried oregano
4 slices of bread (homemade)

1. Preheat oven to 300 degrees.
2. In large mixing bowl, combine oil, garlic powder, celery salt and oregano. Mix with a fork until well combined.
3. Cut each piece of bread into about 16 cubes. Add all the cubes of bread to oil mixture at once. Stir with a rubber spatula so that bread is evenly coated with oil mixture.
4. Place cubes of bread on a cookie sheet and place in preheated oven.
5. Bake approximately 10 to 15 minutes or until croutons are lightly browned and crisp.
6. When croutons are done, remove from oven and let cool completely.
7. Store in airtight container.

This recipe makes approximately 4 cups.

POTATO SALAD

8 cups peeled and diced potatoes
½ cup chopped celery
½ cup chopped green pepper
¼ cup chopped onion
3 hard-boiled eggs, chopped

Dressing:
¾ cup mayonnaise
3 Tablespoons vinegar
2 Tablespoons sugar
1 Tablespoon prepared yellow mustard
1 teaspoon salt
1/8 teaspoon pepper

1. Put potatoes in large soup pot. Add enough water to cover. Bring potatoes to a boil over high heat. Boil 10 minutes or until potatoes are tender. Drain.
2. Transfer boiled potatoes to large mixing bowl. Add celery, green pepper, onion and hard-boiled eggs. Mix and set aside.
3. Make dressing by combining mayonnaise, vinegar, sugar, mustard, salt and pepper in medium mixing bowl. Mix until well combined.
4. Pour dressing over potatoes. Mix until well combined. Chill in refrigerator.

This recipe makes approximately 8 cups.

TUNA MACARONI SALAD

3 cups uncooked elbow macaroni
1 can (6-ounce) tuna, drained
2 cups uncooked frozen peas, thawed
2 Tablespoons chopped onion
1 cup mayonnaise
1 Tablespoon parsley flakes
½ teaspoon salt
1/8 teaspoon pepper

1. Cook elbow macaroni according to package directions.
2. After draining macaroni, rinse with cold water so that noodles are no longer warm.
3. Put cooked macaroni in large mixing bowl. Add tuna, peas, chopped onion, mayonnaise, parsley flakes, salt and pepper.
4. Mix with a spoon until well combined.
5. Chill in refrigerator or serve immediately.

This recipe makes approximately 8 cups.

<u>Recipe Variation</u>:
   Add ½ to 1 cup shredded cheddar cheese.

COLESLAW

2 cups shredded cabbage
½ cup shredded carrot
1 Tablespoon finely chopped onion
¼ cup mayonnaise
1 Tablespoon vinegar
1 teaspoon sugar
½ teaspoon celery salt

1. Place shredded cabbage in large mixing bowl. Add shredded carrot and chopped onion. Mix briefly.
2. In separate bowl, combine mayonnaise, vinegar, sugar and celery salt.
3. Pour mayonnaise mixture over cabbage mixture. Stir until well combined and then refrigerate.

This recipe serves 4.

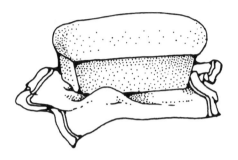

BREADS

There is nothing quite like the smell of homemade bread baking in the oven. Sandwiches taste so much better on homemade white or whole-wheat bread. Making yeast breads is easy for us because we have a heavy-duty mixer, so we don't have to knead the dough by hand. When we make white or whole-wheat bread, we make four loaves at a time. When we make cinnamon-raisin bread, we make two loaves at a time. Cinnamon-raisin bread tastes great toasted for breakfast. Yeast rolls are great served with soups or a casserole. Cornbread goes great with chili. We make banana bread when we have overripe bananas that need to be used. Some of the breads in this section are higher in fat and sugar and shouldn't be made as often. These breads taste great, but are really more like a dessert. For example, apple, banana, rhubarb and zucchini breads.

WHITE BREAD

½ cup water
3 Tablespoons sugar
2 teaspoons salt
3 Tablespoons butter
1½ cups warm water
2 Tablespoons dry yeast
6 cups all-purpose flour

1. Put ½ cup water in saucepan. Add sugar, salt and butter. Heat over medium heat, stirring until butter is completely melted. Remove saucepan from heat and let mixture cool until lukewarm.
2. Put the 1½ cups warm water into mixing bowl of heavy-duty mixer. Add yeast and mix until it dissolves. Let it stand a few minutes so that mixture becomes foamy.
3. Add lukewarm mixture from saucepan to yeast mixture. Mix briefly on low speed with a mixer equipped with dough hook.
4. Add the 6 cups flour and knead with dough hook until dough clings to hook and cleans sides of bowl. Place dough in a lightly greased bowl and let it rise until it doubles in size.
5. Grease two 9-by-5-inch loaf pans.
6. Once dough has doubled, punch it down, divide it in half and roll it out with a rolling pin about ½ inch thick. Try to keep the dough in a rectangular shape. Roll the dough up and form it into a loaf shape. Place in greased loaf pans.
7. Let dough rise again in the loaf pans. Preheat oven to 350 degrees when dough has almost totally risen. (It will be slightly rounded above pans.)

8. When dough has risen, put loaves into preheated oven. Bake 35 minutes. The loaves should be a medium brown when fully baked.
9. Remove them from oven and from pans. Let loaves cool on a wire rack.

Makes 2 loaves.

To make **"WHOLE-WHEAT BREAD"**, *use 2 cups of whole-wheat flour in place of 2 cups of all-purpose flour.*

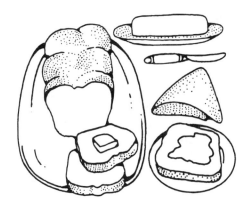

CINNAMON-RAISIN BREAD

1½ Tablespoons butter
2 Tablespoons sugar
1½ Tablespoon instant dry milk
1½ teaspoon salt
2 teaspoon ground cinnamon
1 cup raisins
1¼ cup warm water
1 Tablespoon dry yeast
3½ to 4 cups all-purpose flour

1. Melt butter in saucepan over medium heat. Stir until butter is completely melted. Remove from heat and let it cool until lukewarm.
2. In mixing bowl, combine sugar, dry milk, salt, cinnamon and raisins. Mix with a fork until well combined. Set aside.
3. Put warm water in mixing bowl of heavy-duty mixer. Add yeast and mix until it dissolves.
4. Once yeast dissolves, add lukewarm butter from saucepan to yeast mixture. Mix briefly on low speed with mixer equipped with dough hook. Add sugar-raisin mixture and mix again.
5. Add flour and knead with dough hook until dough clings to hook and cleans sides of bowl. Place dough in a lightly greased bowl and let it rise until it doubles in size.
6. Grease one 9-by-5-inch loaf pan.
7. Once dough has doubled, punch it down and roll it out with a rolling pin about ½ inch thick. Try to keep the dough in a rectangular shape. Roll the dough up and form it into a

loaf shape. Place loaf in greased pan.
8. Let dough rise again in loaf pan. Preheat oven to 350 degrees when the dough has almost totally risen. (It will be slightly rounded above pan.)
9. Bake 35 minutes. The loaf should be a medium brown when fully baked.
10. Remove from oven and from pan. Let loaf cool on a wire rack.

Makes 1 loaf.

PIZZA DOUGH

1 cup warm water
1 Tablespoon dry yeast
½ teaspoon salt
2 teaspoons oil
2½ to 3½ cups flour

1. Put water in mixing bowl of heavy-duty mixer. Add yeast and mix until it dissolves. Let it stand a few minutes so that mixture becomes foamy.
2. Add salt and oil. Mix briefly on low speed with mixer equipped with dough hook.
3. Add 2½ cups flour and knead with dough hook until dough clings to hook and cleans sides of bowl.
4. If dough is too sticky, add more flour and knead again.
5. Place dough in a lightly greased bowl and let it rise until it doubles in size.
6. Grease a 14-inch pizza pan.
7. When dough has doubled in size, punch it down. Press out dough to fit the 14-inch pan.
8. Add desired pizza toppings and bake according to the pizza recipe.

YEAST ROLLS

1½ cups warm water
2 Tablespoons dry yeast
¼ cup sugar
1/3 cup oil
1 egg
1½ teaspoons salt
5 cups all-purpose flour

1. Put water in mixing bowl of heavy-duty mixer. Add yeast and sugar. Mix with a fork until yeast and sugar have dissolved. Let mixture stand a few minutes so that it becomes foamy.
2. Add oil, egg and salt. Mix briefly on low speed with mixer equipped with dough hook.
3. Add the 5 cups flour and knead with dough hook until dough clings to hook and cleans sides of bowl. Place dough in a lightly greased bowl and let it rise until it doubles in size.
4. Grease 24 muffin cups.
5. Once dough has doubled, punch it down. Divide dough evenly among the 24 muffin cups.
6. Let dough rise again in muffin cups. Preheat oven to 400 degrees when dough has almost totally risen.
7. When dough has risen, put muffin pans into preheated oven. Bake 10 to 15 minutes or until rolls are medium brown.
8. When rolls are done, remove them from the oven and take them out of the muffin cups. Let them cool on a wire rack or serve them warm.

Makes 24 rolls.

Recipe Variation:

You can use 2 cups of whole-wheat flour and 3 cups of all-purpose flour instead of 5 cups of all-purpose flour for whole-wheat yeast rolls.

BISCUITS

2 cups flour
4 teaspoons baking powder
1 Tablespoon sugar
½ teaspoon salt
6 Tablespoons butter
2/3 cup milk

1. Preheat oven to 425 degrees.
2. Put flour in large mixing bowl. Add baking powder, sugar and salt. Mix these dry ingredients together with a fork until well combined.
3. Add butter. Cut butter into mixture with a fork or pastry cutter until butter is the size of peas.
4. Add milk. Mix until a dough ball is formed. You may need to use your hands to knead a bit.
5. Place dough on a lightly floured surface. Knead about 10 times. Roll out dough with a rolling pin until dough is approximately ½-inch thick. Cut out biscuits with a round cookie cutter or top of a glass. Reroll and cut the scraps.
6. Place the biscuits on cookie sheet about 2 inches apart. Place cookie sheet in preheated oven and bake approximately 10 to 12 minutes or until biscuits are a light golden brown and well risen.

This recipe makes 16 biscuits.

To make **"CHEDDAR CHEESE BISCUITS,"** *add 2/3 cup grated cheddar cheese at the same time you add the milk.*

APPLE BREAD

2 cups flour
1 teaspoon baking soda
1 teaspoon baking powder
½ teaspoon salt
1 teaspoon ground cinnamon
1 cup sugar
½ cup oil
2 eggs
1 teaspoon vanilla extract
1 cup milk
1½ cups chopped peeled apples

1. Preheat oven to 350 degrees.
2. Put flour in large mixing bowl. Add baking soda, baking powder, salt, cinnamon and sugar. Mix together gently with a fork to combine the dry ingredients.
3. Add oil, eggs, vanilla and milk. Mix together with electric mixer on medium speed until well combined. Scrape sides of the bowl with a rubber spatula if necessary.
4. Peel and cut enough small apple pieces to yield 1½ cups. Add apple pieces to batter and stir in.
5. Grease two 9-by-5-inch loaf pans. Divide batter evenly between the 2 greased pans.
6. Put pans in preheated oven and bake approximately 40 minutes or until bread has browned and a knife inserted into center comes out clean.
7. When loaves are done, remove them from oven and let them cool in pans on a wire rack or on top of the stove.

This recipe makes two loaves, a total of 18 slices.

BANANA BREAD

2 bananas
1 + 1/3 cups sugar
1/3 cup oil
2 eggs
1/3 cup water
1½ cups flour
¼ teaspoon baking powder
1 teaspoon baking soda
½ teaspoon salt

1. Preheat oven to 350 degrees.
2. Peel and put bananas in large mixing bowl. Mash bananas with a fork until they are very mushy.
3. Add sugar, oil, eggs and water. Mix with electric mixer until well combined. Scrape sides of bowl with a rubber spatula if necessary.
4. Add flour, baking powder, baking soda and salt. Mix with an electric mixer until well combined. Scrape sides of bowl with a rubber spatula if necessary.
5. Grease two 9-by-5-inch loaf pans. Divide batter evenly between the 2 greased pans.
6. Put pans in preheated oven and bake approximately 40 minutes or until loaves are a medium brown and knife inserted into center comes out clean.
7. When loaves are done, remove them from oven and let them cool in pans on a wire rack or on top of the stove.

This recipe makes 2 loaves, a total of 18 slices.

To make **"PUMPKIN BREAD,"** *substitute 1 cup of solid pack pumpkin and ½ teaspoon cinnamon for the bananas.*

CORNBREAD

1 cup yellow cornmeal
1 cup flour
2 Tablespoons sugar (optional)
1 Tablespoon baking powder
½ teaspoon salt
1 cup milk
1 egg
¼ cup oil

1. Preheat oven to 400 degrees.
2. Put cornmeal in large mixing bowl. Add flour, sugar if using, baking powder and salt. Mix with a fork to combine these dry ingredients.
3. Add milk, egg and oil. Mix with a fork to combine all ingredients. Scrape sides of bowl with a rubber spatula if necessary.
4. Grease 8 or 9-inch square baking pan. Pour and spread batter evenly into pan.
5. Put pan in preheated oven and bake approximately 20 to 25 minutes or until a knife inserted into center comes out clean and bread is golden.
6. When bread is done, remove pan from oven and let it cool on a wire rack or on top of the stove. You can also serve this bread warm. Cut into squares.

This recipe makes 9 to 12 servings.

You can also make this bread into 12 muffins by pouring the batter into 12 greased muffin cups and baking for approximately 15 to 20 minutes or until golden and a toothpick inserted in the center comes out clean.

RHUBARB BREAD

1 cup milk
1 Tablespoon vinegar
1½ cups sugar
2/3 cup oil
1 egg
1 teaspoon vanilla extract
½ teaspoon salt
1 teaspoon baking soda
2¾ cups flour
1½ cups chopped rhubarb

1. Preheat oven to 350 degrees.
2. Combine milk and vinegar in small mixing bowl. Set aside.
3. Put sugar in large mixing bowl. Add oil, egg, vanilla, salt and baking soda. Mix with an electric mixer until well combined. Scrape sides of bowl with a rubber spatula if necessary.
4. Add flour and milk/vinegar combination. Mix with electric mixer until well combined. Scrape sides of bowl with a rubber spatula if necessary.
5. Add rhubarb and mix again with electric mixer.
6. Grease two 9-by-5-inch loaf pans. Divide batter evenly between the 2 greased pans.
7. Put pans in preheated oven and bake for approximately 50 minutes or until loaves are lightly browned and a knife inserted into center comes out clean.
8. When loaves are done, remove them from oven and let them cool in pans on a wire rack or on top of stove.

This recipe makes 2 loaves, a total of 18 slices.

ZUCCHINI BREAD

2 cups grated zucchini
3 eggs
2 cups sugar
1 cup oil
1 Tablespoon vanilla extract
3 cups flour
1 teaspoon salt
1 teaspoon baking soda
½ teaspoon baking powder
½ Tablespoon ground cinnamon

1. Preheat oven to 325 degrees.
2. Grate enough zucchini to yield 2 cups. You don't need to peel zucchini first. Set aside.
3. Break 3 eggs into large mixing bowl. Add sugar, oil and vanilla. Mix with electric mixer until well combined. Add zucchini and mix again. Scrape sides of bowl with a rubber spatula if necessary.
4. Combine flour, salt, baking soda, baking powder and cinnamon in a separate bowl.
5. Add dry ingredients to the zucchini mixture. Mix with electric mixer until completely combined. Scrape sides of bowl with a rubber spatula if necessary.
6. Grease three 9-by-5-inch loaf pans. Divide batter evenly among the 3 greased pans.
7. Bake in preheated oven approximately 60 minutes or until loaves are medium brown and a knife inserted into center comes out clean.
8. When loaves are done, remove them from oven and let them cool in pans on a wire rack or on top of stove.
   This recipe makes 3 loaves, a total of 27 slices.

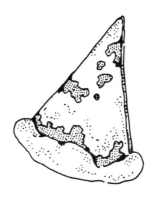

DINNER

We know that people today lead very active lives. Careers and outside activities keep people very busy. Preparing a good dinner is something many people choose not to make the time for. Some feel it is too boring or troublesome. Others don't want it to interrupt what they consider to be a more important, interesting project. Convenient alternatives to spending time in the kitchen include fast food restaurants and TV dinners. These people don't realize how important nutritious home-cooked meals are. Nutrition is the key to a healthy family, and nutritious home cooking is easier than you think.

Avoiding restaurants is a big money saver. It is much

cheaper to eat at home. Let's say we take our family of seven to McDonald's for dinner and spend $25. We could make dinner at home for less than $5. Is the convenience of not having to cook worth $20 to us? No, it is not. For one thing, going out to eat with five kids is rarely fun or easier than cooking at home. Secondly, the price paid for this convenience amounts to a reduction in available nutrients.

The same can be said about a take-out pizza or frozen pizza. Getting two large take-out cheese pizzas might cost $15. Buying enough frozen pizza to feed our family might run $10. But making two of our homemade pizzas will cost less than $5. Our pizza tastes really good and doesn't take much hands-on preparation time. Our advice is to calculate the cost of the convenience of going out to eat or of buying prepackaged convenience food. Is it worth it to your family? To us, it is not worth it. We enjoy our diet and don't miss dining out. There is no deprivation-- only our family reaching our financial goals sooner. It is amazing how much money you can save when you choose to cook meals at home from scratch. This is something to think about if you are dreaming about early retirement or wondering how you are going to pay for your kids' college educations.

Another way to save on your grocery bill is to eat less meat. Meat can be a very expensive food, and Americans eat too much of it. Over consumption of animal products is linked to many health problems, cancer and heart disease being the two big ones.

We are all being told to decrease our intake of saturated fats and increase our intake of fiber. Well, guess what is very high in saturated fat and low in fiber? Meat! Saturated fats are a factor associated with high cholesterol levels and heart disease. Most Americans need to cut down on fat and cholesterol and increase fiber. Cholesterol is not found in plant food. Meat, fish and dairy foods are the only sources of dietary cholesterol.

Not only is eating a lot of meat bad for our health and wallet, but it also is bad for the environment. Plant-based foods don't harm the environment as much as meat-based foods because they use less energy to produce. Meat-oriented diets are extremely wasteful to our land, water and forests. Consuming animal products plays a role in the destruction of our forests, topsoil and the using up of our water. We have a responsibility to the world, not just ourselves. Our excess meat consumption is not fair to future generations or to the Earth.

We don't eat any beef at our house. We use some chicken and turkey. We also use some tuna. On many days we have no meat at all. Based on physiology, human beings are biologically adapted to eat food from the plant kingdom. All you have to do is compare our digestive tracts to those of meat-eating animals and plant-eating animals. You will see that ours is nothing like meat eaters but very similar to plant eaters.

We are not suggesting that in order to be healthy, you have to be a vegetarian. What we are suggesting is that you should eat less meat and more unprocessed plant foods if you currently eat a lot of meat. You don't need to be a complete vegetarian who never eats meat again, but vegetarianism should be a part of your dietary lifestyle.

When we do use meat, we try not to make it the center of the meal but rather add a little to a casserole or view it as a side dish instead. Use meats as flavoring, not as the main dish.

To change your meat-eating habits, try cutting out meat some of the days of the week. At least try to lower your overall consumption. If you eat a typical American diet, you will not have a protein deficiency if you cut back on your meat intake.

So to sum it up, you are wasting money if you are eating dinner often at restaurants or buying lots of convenience food for this meal. If you feel that preparing dinner takes too much of your time or is too boring or troublesome, we urge you to change your priorities. Nutritious home-cooked meals are just too important not to make the time for. If your career keeps you very busy, then work around your busy schedule. You can make many of these meals ahead of time and put them in the oven when you get home from work. Other meals that you can make ahead just need to be reheated when you get home. Save recipes that take longer to prepare for your days off. Spaghetti is always a good meal when you are rushed for time.

CHEESY PIZZA

"PIZZA DOUGH" (see recipe on page 63)
1 can (8-ounce) of tomato sauce
1 teaspoon dried oregano
1 teaspoon dried basil
¼ teaspoon garlic powder
1/8 teaspoon pepper
2 cups shredded mozzarella cheese

1. Prepare **"PIZZA DOUGH"** recipe.
2. Preheat oven to 400 degrees.
3. To make pizza sauce, combine tomato sauce, oregano, basil, garlic powder and pepper in small mixing bowl.
4. Spread pizza sauce evenly over pizza dough.
5. Sprinkle mozzarella cheese evenly over pizza sauce.
6. Bake pizza in preheated oven approximately 15 to 20 minutes or until pizza dough is light to medium brown and cheese has melted and browned.
7. When pizza is done, remove it from oven. Let cool briefly, then remove pizza from pan and cut into wedges..

This recipe makes 8 slices.

<u>Recipe Variations:</u>
Sometimes when we have leftover spaghetti sauce, we will use ½ to 1 cup of that instead of the pizza sauce. You can also top the pizza with other ingredients like chopped onion, green pepper, cooked meat, etc. Add these ingredients before you add the cheese.

SOUTHWESTERN-STYLE PIZZA

"PIZZA DOUGH" (see recipe on page 63)
1 cup refried beans
½ Tablespoon chili powder
1/8 teaspoon ground cumin
1/8 teaspoon onion powder
1/8 teaspoon garlic powder
¼ teaspoon salt
¼ cup chopped green pepper
¼ cup chopped onion
1 cup shredded cheddar cheese
1 cup shredded mozzarella cheese

1. Prepare "PIZZA DOUGH" recipe.
2. Preheat oven to 400 degrees.
3. Put refried beans into small mixing bowl. Add chili powder, cumin, onion powder, garlic powder and salt. Mix these ingredients until well combined.
4. Spread refried bean mixture evenly over pizza dough.
5. Sprinkle chopped green pepper and chopped onion evenly over refried bean mixture.
6. Sprinkle shredded cheddar and shredded mozzarella evenly over pizza.
7. Bake pizza in preheated oven approximately 15 to 20 minutes or until pizza dough is light to medium brown and cheese has melted and browned.
8. When pizza is done, remove it from oven. Let cool briefly, then remove pizza from pan and cut into wedges.

This recipe makes 8 slices.

TUNA NOODLE CASSEROLE

1 bag (12-ounce) egg noodles
2 cans (10¾-ounce) condensed cream of mushroom soup
2 cups milk
1 can (6-ounce) tuna
2 cups frozen peas
2 cups shredded cheddar cheese

1. Cook noodles according to package directions.
2. Preheat oven to 350 degrees.
3. Grease large casserole dish.
4. Add cream of mushroom soup and milk to casserole dish. Stir with whisk until well combined.
5. Drain tuna. Add to casserole. Mix tuna with milk and soup.
6. Add peas, shredded cheese and drained noodles to other ingredients. Mix with spoon until completely mixed.
7. Cover casserole and bake in preheated oven approximately 30 minutes or until casserole is bubbly and cheese has melted. Serve immediately.

*This recipe makes approximately
10 cups or 8 servings.*

TUNA AND RICE CASSEROLE

2 cups rice
4 cups water
2 cans (10¾-ounce) condensed cream of mushroom soup
2 teaspoons salt
1/8 teaspoon pepper
2 cups frozen peas
1 can (6-ounce) of tuna, drained
2 cups shredded cheddar cheese

1. Preheat oven to 350 degrees.
2. Lightly grease large casserole dish.
3. Put rice in casserole dish. Add water, cream of mushroom soup, salt, pepper, peas, tuna and cheese. Stir until well combined.
4. Cover casserole dish and bake in preheated oven approximately 1 to 1½ hours. Casserole is done when it is no longer soupy and rice is tender.

This recipe makes approximately
10 cups or 8 servings.

Recipe Variation:
You can substitute brown rice in this recipe. However, the cooking time will increase by about ½ hour.

CABBAGE CASSEROLE

1 pound ground turkey
6 cups chopped cabbage
1 cup chopped onion
1 can (10¾-ounce) condensed tomato soup
1 cup water
4 Tablespoons uncooked rice
1 teaspoon salt
1/8 teaspoon pepper

1. Preheat oven to 350 degrees.
2. Brown meat in skillet over medium heat, stirring until crumbly. Drain off any fat.
3. Put chopped cabbage in casserole dish. Add onion, tomato soup, water, rice, salt, pepper and the cooked ground meat. Stir until well combined.
4. Cover casserole dish and bake in preheated oven approximately 60 minutes. Casserole is done when cabbage is tender.
5. Remove from oven and serve immediately.

*This recipe makes approximately
6 cups or 6 servings.*

MEATLOAF

Loaf:
1 pound ground turkey
1 cup rolled oats
1 cup chopped onion
½ cup tomato sauce
1 egg
1 teaspoon salt
¼ teaspoon pepper

Sauce:
½ cup water
½ cup tomato sauce
2 Tablespoons brown sugar, packed
2 Tablespoons prepared yellow mustard
1 Tablespoon vinegar

1. Preheat oven to 350 degrees.
2. Put ground turkey in large mixing bowl. Add oats, onion, ½ cup tomato sauce, egg, salt and pepper. Mix with fork until thoroughly combined. Press meatloaf into 9-by-5¼-inch loaf pan.
3. In small mixing bowl, combine ½ cup tomato sauce, brown sugar, yellow mustard and vinegar. Mix together with a fork or a whisk until completely mixed. Pour over meatloaf.
4. Bake in preheated oven approximately 60 minutes.
5. Remove from oven and serve immediately.

This recipe makes approximately 6 servings.

OVEN-ROASTED POTATO FRIES

6 large baking potatoes (unpeeled)
3 Tablespoons oil
¼ teaspoon dried thyme
¼ teaspoon dried rosemary
¼ teaspoon paprika
¼ teaspoon salt
1/8 teaspoon pepper

1. Preheat oven to 425 degrees.
2. Wash and cut each potato into 8 wedges.
3. Put potato wedges in 13-by-9-inch pan.
4. In small mixing bowl, combine oil, thyme, rosemary, paprika, salt and pepper. Stir until well combined.
5. Drizzle oil mixture evenly over potatoes, using rubber spatula to get last bit of oil out of bowl.
6. Mix oil mixture and potatoes with spatula in pan so the potatoes are evenly coated.
7. Cover pan with aluminum foil. Bake in preheated oven 45 minutes.
8. Remove them from oven and take off the aluminum foil.
9. Flip potatoes with firm spatula and return them to the oven uncovered.
10. Bake additional 20 minutes or until potato fries are done.

This recipe makes 6 servings.

PORCUPINE MEAT BALLS

1 pound ground turkey
½ cup uncooked rice
½ cup chopped onion
2 Tablespoons ketchup
1½ teaspoons salt
1 can (10¾-ounce) condensed tomato soup

1. Preheat oven to 350 degrees.
2. Put ground turkey in mixing bowl. Add rice, onion, ketchup and salt. Mix these ingredients together with a fork until well combined.
3. Shape mixture into 12 meatballs and place in casserole dish in one layer. Pour tomato soup over meatballs.
4. Cover casserole dish and bake in preheated oven approximately 60 minutes or until done.

This recipe makes 4 to 6 servings.

MASHED POTATOES

8 cups peeled and chopped potatoes
1 teaspoon salt
½ cup milk
2 Tablespoons butter
Salt and pepper to taste

1. Put potatoes in soup pot. Pour in enough water to cover potatoes. Add salt.
2. Bring the potatoes to a boil over high heat.
3. When water is boiling, reduce heat to medium and continue boiling potatoes 15 to 20 minutes or until potatoes are soft.
4. Drain potatoes and place in large mixing bowl. Add milk and butter.
5. Mix potatoes with an electric mixer on medium or high speed until all the potatoes are mashed and there are no lumps.

This recipe serves 6 to 8.

SIX LAYER CASSEROLE

1 pound ground turkey
2 cups diced potatoes
2 cups chopped carrots
½ cup uncooked rice
1 cup chopped onion
2 cans (14.5-ounce) whole peeled tomatoes, chopped
1 teaspoon salt
1/8 teaspoon pepper

1. Preheat oven to 300 degrees.
2. Brown turkey in skillet over medium heat, stirring until crumbly. Drain off any fat.
3. Place potatoes in large casserole dish. Add carrots, rice, onion, ground meat, tomatoes, layering in order. Add salt and pepper.
4. Cover casserole dish and bake in preheated oven approximately 2 hours, stirring about halfway through baking time.
5. Remove from oven and serve immediately.

This recipe makes approximately
7 cups or 6 servings.

CHICKEN STIR-FRY

1½ cups sliced carrots
½ cup chopped celery
1 cup chopped onion
2 cups frozen broccoli
1 cup frozen peas
1 cup leftover chicken or turkey, cut up
1½ cups water
2 teaspoons garlic powder
1 Tablespoon vegetable-flavored bouillon granules
½ cup soy sauce
4 Tablespoons flour

1. In large saucepan, combine carrots, celery, onion, broccoli, peas, chicken, water, garlic powder and vegetable bouillon granules.
2. Bring mixture to a boil over high heat, stirring constantly.
3. When mixture is boiling, reduce heat to low and cover saucepan. Simmer 15 to 20 minutes.
4. While mixture simmers, pour soy sauce into bowl. Add flour and stir until flour has dissolved.
5. After the vegetable/meat mixture has simmered, add soy sauce mixture. Cook, stirring, until sauce has thickened. Serve over rice.

This recipe makes six servings.

We cook enough rice to yield approximately 6 cups and make sure the rice gets done at the same time as the chicken stir-fry.

To make **"VEGETABLE STIR-FRY,"** *omit the meat and add 1 cup of the vegetable of your choice.*

TACO BAKE

"BISCUITS" (see recipe on page 65)
1 pound ground turkey
1 cup chopped onion
½ cup chopped green pepper
1 teaspoon salt
1/8 teaspoon pepper
1 Tablespoon chili powder
1 can (6-ounce) tomato paste
¾ cup water
1 cup grated cheddar cheese

1. Prepare "BISCUITS" recipe, skipping steps 5 and 6. Press dough into bottom of a 13-by-9-inch pan.
2. Preheat oven to 400 degrees.
3. Put ground turkey in frying pan. Add onion and green pepper. Brown meat over medium heat, stirring until crumbly. Drain off any fat.
4. Add salt, pepper, chili powder, tomato paste and water. Stir until well combined.
5. Spread mixture over biscuit dough in pan.
6. Sprinkle grated cheddar cheese on top.
7. Bake in preheated oven approximately 15 minutes or until crust has browned.
8. Remove from oven. Cut it into 8 pieces and serve immediately.

This recipe makes 8 servings.

ENCHILADAS

1 pound ground turkey
1 can (14.5-ounce) whole peeled tomatoes, chopped
1 can (6-ounce) tomato paste
½ cup water
1 cup chopped onion
1 Tablespoon chili powder
1¼ teaspoon salt
¼ teaspoon pepper
10 soft flour tortilla shells
2 cups grated cheddar cheese

1. Brown meat in skillet over medium heat, stirring until crumbly. Drain off any fat.
2. Add tomatoes, tomato paste, water, onion, chili powder, salt and pepper. Mix until well combined.
3. Turn heat on high and bring mixture to a boil. When mixture is boiling, reduce heat to low, cover and simmer 15 minutes.
4. Remove pan from heat. Preheat oven to 350 degrees.
5. Prepare each enchilada by adding ¼ cup sauce and 1/8 cup grated cheese to middle of each tortilla shell. Roll up each tortilla shell and line up side by side, seam side down, in 13-by-9-inch pan.
6. Spread remaining sauce evenly over enchiladas. Top with remaining grated cheese. Cover with aluminum foil.
7. Bake in preheated oven approximately 30 minutes or until done. They will be done when cheese has melted and bottoms of tortilla shells have browned.
8. Remove from oven and serve immediately.

This recipe makes 10 enchiladas.

BURRITOS

1 Tablespoon oil
2 cups chopped onion
1 cup chopped green pepper
1 Tablespoon minced garlic
½ teaspoon salt
¼ teaspoon garlic powder
¼ teaspoon onion powder
¼ teaspoon ground cumin
1 Tablespoon chili powder
1 can (16-ounce) refried beans
10 soft flour tortilla shells
Oil for frying

1. Put the 1 Tablespoon oil into frying pan. Add onions, green pepper and garlic. Saute over medium heat, stirring often, until onions and green peppers are tender. (Add a little water if they start to burn or dry out too much).
2. Remove from heat. Add salt, garlic powder, onion powder, cumin and chili powder. Stir. Add refried beans. Stir until mixture is well combined.
3. Add ¼ cup filling to center of a tortilla shell. Fold left and right sides over a bit and then fold bottom over top. Place on a plate with the folded side down. Repeat until filling is gone and all tortilla shells are used.
4. Pour ½ cup oil into electric frying pan. Set at 350 degrees. When oil is hot, fry tortillas on both sides, folded side down first, until both sides are brown. You may need to add a little more oil after about half are done.
5. Place fried burritos on plate with paper towel so that some of the oil can be absorbed.

This recipe makes 10 burritos.

TACOS

Meat filling:
1 pound ground turkey
1 cup chopped onion
½ cup chopped green pepper
1 teaspoon salt
1/8 teaspoon pepper
1 Tablespoon chili powder
1 can (6-ounce) tomato paste
¾ cup water

Tacos:
10 soft flour tortillas
Meat filling
Shredded lettuce
Shredded cheddar cheese
Sliced tomatoes
Sour cream

1. Place ground turkey in frying pan. Add onion and green pepper. Brown meat over medium heat, stirring until crumbly. Drain off any fat.
2. Add salt, pepper, chili powder, tomato paste and water. Stir until well combined. Simmer over low heat while heating tortillas.
3. Heat tortillas according to package directions.
4. Make tacos by placing some of the meat filling down center of a warm tortilla. Top with shredded lettuce, shredded cheese, sliced tomatoes and sour cream.
5. Fold two sides of tortilla so they overlap.

This recipe makes 10 tacos.

MEXICALI CASSEROLE

1 cup uncooked rice
1 can (15-ounce) kidney beans
2 cups corn
2 cans (14.5-ounce) whole peeled tomatoes, chopped
1 to 2 cups chopped onion
2 cups water
1 teaspoon salt
1/8 teaspoon pepper
1 teaspoon chili powder

1. Preheat oven to 350 degrees.
2. Lightly grease large casserole dish.
3. Put rice in casserole dish. Add kidney beans, corn, tomatoes, onion, water, salt, pepper and chili powder.
4. Stir these ingredients until well combined.
5. Cover casserole dish and bake in preheated oven approximately 1½ hours or until casserole is no longer soupy and rice is tender.

This recipe makes approximately
8 cups or 6 to 8 servings.

Recipe Variations:
You can use brown rice instead of white. If you do, the cooking time will increase by approximately ½ hour.

You might want to add 1 chopped green pepper to this casserole.

CHILI

1 pound ground turkey
1 cup chopped onion
½ cup chopped green pepper (optional)
½ cup chopped celery
2 cans (14.5-ounce) whole peeled tomatoes, chopped
1 can (6-ounce) tomato paste
4 cups water (divided)
2 teaspoons salt
¼ teaspoon pepper
3 teaspoons chili powder
1 teaspoon garlic powder
1 cup dry elbow macaroni
2 cans (15-ounce) kidney beans

1. Brown turkey in skillet over medium heat, stirring until crumbly. Drain off any fat.
2. Place meat in large soup pot. Add onion, green pepper if using, celery, tomatoes, tomato paste, 2 cups water, salt, pepper, chili powder and garlic powder. Stir until well combined.
3. Bring chili to a boil over high heat.
4. When chili is boiling, reduce heat to low, cover and simmer 30 minutes.
5. While chili simmers, cook elbow macaroni according to package directions.
6. After chili has simmered 30 minutes, add cooked macaroni, kidney beans and remaining 2 cups water.
7. Return chili to a boil, then simmer covered additional 15 minutes.

This recipe makes approximately 14 cups.

SLOPPY JOES

1 pound ground turkey
1 cup chopped onion
½ cup chopped green pepper
2 teaspoons soy sauce
1 teaspoon chili powder
½ teaspoon salt
1/8 teaspoon pepper
1 cup tomato sauce
8 hamburger buns

1. Place ground turkey in frying pan. Add onion and green
    pepper. Brown meat over medium heat, stirring until
    crumbly. Drain off any fat.
2. Add soy sauce, chili powder, salt, pepper and tomato
    sauce. Stir until well combined.
3. Bring mixture to a boil, then reduce heat to low, cover and
    simmer 30 to 50 minutes to let flavors blend. Serve on
    buns.

This recipe makes 2½ to 3 cups, about 8 servings.

SPAGHETTI SAUCE

1 cup chopped onion
1 Tablespoon minced garlic
1/3 cup chopped celery
1 can (6-ounce) tomato paste
2 cans (14.5-ounce) whole peeled tomatoes, chopped
1 cup water
1 Tablespoon salt
1 Tablespoon sugar
¼ teaspoon pepper
1/8 teaspoon dried oregano
1/8 teaspoon chili powder
¼ teaspoon dried thyme
2 Tablespoons parsley flakes
1 bay leaf

1. In large soup pot, combine onion, garlic, celery, tomato paste, tomatoes and water. Add salt, sugar, pepper, oregano, chili powder, thyme, parsley flakes and bay leaf. Stir until combined.
2. Cover and bring mixture to a boil over high heat. Stir.
3. Reduce heat and simmer, covered for 3 hours, stirring occasionally.
4. Remove bay leaf before serving.

This recipe makes approximately 4 cups sauce.

SPINACH LASAGNA

1½ cups chopped onion
2 cans (14.5-ounce) whole peeled tomatoes, chopped
½ teaspoon salt
½ teaspoon garlic powder
1/8 teaspoon pepper
1½ teaspoons dried oregano
1 cup water
9 lasagna noodles, uncooked
1 package (10-ounce) frozen spinach
1 package (16-ounce) shredded mozzarella cheese

1. In soup pot, combine onion, chopped tomatoes, salt, garlic powder, pepper, oregano and water.
2. Bring tomato sauce to a boil over high heat.
3. When tomato sauce is boiling, reduce heat to low and simmer uncovered 20 to 30 minutes.
4. Preheat oven to 350 degrees.
5. Pour 1 cup of the tomato sauce in bottom of 13-by-9-inch pan. Lay 3 lasagna noodles side by side on top of sauce. Spread 1/3 of package of spinach on top of lasagna noodles. Sprinkle 1/3 of the cheese on top of spinach.
6. Repeat this process 2 more times.
7. Pour any remaining sauce over top. Cover with aluminum foil and bake in preheated oven 45 minutes. Remove aluminum foil and bake uncovered additional 15 minutes.
8. Remove from oven and let lasagna sit about 15 minutes to set.

This recipe makes 8 servings.

LASAGNA

1 pound ground turkey
1 cup chopped onion
2 cans (14.5-ounce) whole peeled tomatoes, chopped
1 can (6-ounce) tomato paste
1 Tablespoon parsley flakes
½ teaspoon rosemary
½ teaspoon basil
½ teaspoon oregano
½ teaspoon salt
½ teaspoon garlic powder
1/8 teaspoon pepper
9 lasagna noodles
1 package (16-ounce) shredded mozzarella cheese

1. Put ground turkey in soup pot. Add onion. Brown meat over medium heat, stirring until crumbly. Drain off any fat.
2. Add tomatoes, tomato paste, parsley, rosemary, basil, oregano, salt, garlic powder and pepper. Stir until well combined.
3. Bring mixture to a boil over high heat. When mixture is boiling, cover pot and reduce heat to low and simmer 20 to 30 minutes.
4. Preheat oven to 350 degrees.
5. Cook lasagna noodles according to package directions.
6. When noodles are done and sauce has simmered, lay 3 lasagna noodles side by side in bottom of 13-by-9-inch pan. Add 1½ cups of sauce to noodles. Then sprinkle 1/3 of the cheese on top of sauce. Repeat this process 2 more times.
7. Bake lasagna in preheated oven, uncovered, for 30 minutes.

8. When lasagna is done, remove from oven and let rest 10 minutes before cutting.

This recipe makes 8 servings.

BAKED POTATOES

---

1 medium potato per person

1. Scrub potatoes with vegetable scrubber under running water.
2. Poke holes into potatoes with fork to allow steam to escape.
3. Bake potatoes in oven when baking a main dish such as meatloaf or Mexicali casserole. Potatoes are done when they are soft in the middle. This will take approximately 70 to 80 minutes at 350 degrees or 40 to 60 minutes at 425 degrees.

VEGETABLE LO MEIN

½ pound broken spaghetti
1 cup chopped carrots
3 cups chopped broccoli
2 Tablespoons oil
¼ cup chopped onion
1 cup chopped zucchini
3 cups chopped cabbage
¼ cup soy sauce
½ cup water
1 Tablespoon vegetable-flavored bouillon granules
1 teaspoon garlic powder

1. Cook spaghetti according to package directions. Drain and set aside.
2. Put carrots and broccoli in medium saucepan. Cover with water and boil until tender/crisp, approximately 5 minutes. Drain and set aside.
3. Pour oil into wok or soup pot. Add onion, zucchini and cabbage. Stir-fry over medium heat until vegetables are tender/crisp. Add a little water if vegetables begin to stick.
4. In medium mixing bowl, combine soy sauce, water, vegetable-flavored bouillon and garlic powder. Stir with a spoon until well combined.
5. Pour soy sauce mixture into pot with zucchini and cabbage. Bring to a boil. Add broccoli, carrots and spaghetti. Mix until well combined. Cook 1 minute. Serve immediately.

This recipe makes 6 servings.

GARBANZO BEANS OVER RICE

2 cans (16-ounce) garbanzo beans (or 3 cups cooked)
1 Tablespoon minced garlic
1 cup chopped onion
2 cans (14.5-ounce) whole peeled tomatoes, chopped
1 teaspoon salt
1/8 teaspoon pepper
1 Tablespoon parsley flakes

1.   Put garbanzo beans in large soup pot. Add garlic, onion, tomatoes, salt, pepper and parsley flakes. Stir until well combined.
2.   Over high heat, bring the garbanzo beans to a boil.
3.   When mixture is boiling, reduce heat and simmer 20 to 30 minutes. Garbanzo beans are done when onions are tender. Serve over rice.

*This recipe makes approximately 6 cups
bean mixture, enough for 8 servings.*

*We cook enough rice to yield approximately 9 cups and we make
sure the rice gets done at the same time as the garbanzo beans.*

CHICKEN POT PIE

"9-INCH DOUBLE PIE CRUST" (see recipe on page 119)
1 cup peeled and chopped carrots
1 cup peeled and diced potatoes
½ cup chopped celery
1 cup chopped onion
1 cup frozen green peas
1 cup leftover cooked chicken or turkey, cut up
1 can (10¾-ounce) condensed cream of mushroom soup

1. Prepare a **"9-INCH DOUBLE PIE CRUST."**
2. Put carrots in large soup pot. Add potatoes, celery and onion. Add enough water to cover. Bring vegetables to a boil.
3. When vegetables are boiling, reduce heat and simmer 10 minutes. Preheat oven to 375 degrees.
4. After vegetables have simmered 10 minutes, add peas and chicken. Return to a boil, then drain.
5. Place drained vegetables in large mixing bowl. Add cream of mushroom soup. Mix until well combined. Pour mixture into unbaked pie crust.
6. Add top pie crust and pinch bottom crust and top crust together with a fork around edge of pie pan. Poke approximately 6 vents in top of pie crust with a knife to let steam out.
7. Bake pie in preheated oven approximately 40 minutes or until pie crust is golden brown.
8. Remove from oven and let cool a few minutes. Cut it into 8 pieces and serve.

This recipe makes 8 servings.

To make "VEGETABLE POT PIE," eliminate the chicken and add an extra cup of diced potatoes.

SPINACH CALZONES

"PIZZA DOUGH" (see recipe on page 63)
1 package (10-ounce) frozen spinach, thawed
1½ cups spaghetti sauce
1 bag (16-ounce) grated mozzarella cheese

1. Prepare a double batch of the "PIZZA DOUGH" recipe, eliminating steps 5, 6 and 7.
2. Put spinach in large mixing bowl. Add spaghetti sauce and mozzarella cheese. Stir with a spoon until well mixed.
3. When pizza dough has risen, punch it down and divide it into 14 dough balls.
4. On floured surface, roll each dough ball out to make a circle about 6-inches in diameter.. Add 1/3 cup of filling to center of each dough circle.
5. Wet edges of dough with water, then fold one end over to other end. Seal calzone by pressing edges together with a fork.
6. Repeat until all 14 calzones are done.
7. Preheat oven to 400 degrees. (Freeze calzones you are not planning on baking.) Place calzones on cookie sheet.
8. Bake calzones 15 to 20 minutes or until they are light to medium brown.

This recipe makes 14 calzones.

When using frozen calzones, let them thaw for about 30 minutes on cookie sheet, then bake as usual.

SOUTHWESTERN CALZONES

"PIZZA DOUGH" (see recipe on page 63)
1 Tablespoon oil
2 cups chopped onion
1 cup chopped green pepper
1 Tablespoon minced garlic
½ teaspoon salt
¼ teaspoon garlic powder
¼ teaspoon onion powder
¼ teaspoon ground cumin
1 Tablespoon chili powder
1 can (16-ounce) refried beans

1. Prepare **"PIZZA DOUGH"** recipe, eliminating steps 5, 6 and 7.
2. Pour oil into a frying pan. Add onions, green pepper and garlic. Saute over medium heat, stirring often, until onions and green pepper are tender. (Add a little water if they start to burn or dry out too much).
3. Remove from heat. Add salt, garlic powder, onion powder, cumin and chili powder. Stir. Add refried beans. Stir until mixture is well combined.
4. When pizza dough has risen, punch it down and divide it into 7 dough balls.
5. On floured surface, roll each dough ball out to make a circle about 6-inches in diameter. Add 1/3 cup of filling in center of each dough circle.
6. Wet edges of dough with water, then fold one end over to other end. Seal calzone by pressing edges together with a fork.

7. Repeat until all 7 calzones are done.
8. Preheat oven to 400 degrees. (Freeze calzones you are not planning on baking.) Place calzones on cookie sheet.
9. Bake 15 to 20 minutes or until calzones are light to medium brown.

This recipe makes 7 calzones.

When using frozen calzones, let them thaw for about 30 minutes on cookie sheet, then bake as usual.

BROCCOLI-POTATO-CHICKEN DISH

4 cups peeled and diced potatoes
1 package (16-ounce) frozen broccoli
1 cup leftover cooked chicken, cut up
1 cup shredded cheddar cheese
1 can (10¾-ounce) condensed cream of mushroom soup

1. Preheat oven to 350 degrees.
2. Put potatoes in large casserole dish. Add broccoli, chicken, cheese and cream of mushroom soup. Mix together all ingredients.
3. Cover casserole and place in preheated oven. Bake 1 to 1½ hours, stirring about halfway through cooking time. When potatoes are soft, casserole is done.

This recipe makes approximately 6 cups,
about 4 to 6 servings.

DESSERTS

If you truly want to save money on your grocery bill, don't buy prepackaged snacks and desserts--make them yourself. Our desserts are a lot less expensive than buying prepackaged sweets in the grocery store. That is because when you buy all those prepackaged goodies, you are paying not only for someone else to make the desserts for you, but also for a portion of the advertising and the product's packaging. Another reason to make your own desserts is to avoid the chemicals, dyes, additives and preservatives so often found in desserts bought from stores.

Another suggestion we need to make is to cut back on the total number of snacks and desserts you give your family. As a nation we consume way too many sweets. Sugar has absolutely no nutrients, just calories. Worse, sugar uses up vitamins and minerals when it is metabolized. When you eat foods high in sugar, you probably overeat to obtain the nutrients you need.

Why don't you adopt this family policy? Give your family a sugary snack only after a good meal. If they have an empty stomach between meals, give them something nutritious such as a piece of fruit or a sandwich.

You are not denying your children anything when you say no to a sugary snack. You are in fact letting them know just how much you love them. Cut down on chips of all kinds, soda pop, candy, etc. . . .Your family doesn't benefit in the least by consuming these foods. Remember that too much junk food is not good for you, so eat these types of food in moderation.

On the following pages are the desserts we make for our family. Enjoy them - they taste really good.

OATMEAL COOKIES

¾ cup butter
1 cup brown sugar, packed
½ cup granulated sugar
1 egg
¼ cup water
1 teaspoon vanilla extract
1 teaspoon salt
½ teaspoon baking soda
1 cup flour
3 cups quick-cooking rolled oats
½ cup raisins (optional)

1. Let butter soften to room temperature.
2. Preheat oven to 350 degrees.
3. Place butter in large mixing bowl. Add sugars. Mix on medium or high speed with an electric mixer until creamy. Use a rubber spatula to scrape sides of bowl if necessary.
4. Add egg, water and vanilla. Mix with an electric mixer on medium speed until well blended.
5. Add salt and baking soda and mix again with electric mixer. Beat in flour. Add oats and mix until well blended. Add raisins and mix with a spoon.
6. Drop 12 heaping teaspoons of the cookie dough on cookie sheet approximately 2 inches apart. Place cookie sheet in preheated oven and bake approximately 12 to 15 minutes or until cookies are light to medium brown.
7. When done, remove cookies with a metal spatula and place on a wire rack or a cut open brown paper bag to cool. Store in airtight container.

This recipe makes about 3 dozen cookies.

BANANA COOKIES

2 bananas
1 cup sugar
¾ cup butter
1 teaspoon vanilla extract
2 eggs
2 teaspoons baking powder
½ teaspoon salt
¼ teaspoon baking soda
2½ cups flour

1. Preheat oven to 350 degrees.
2. Peel and place bananas in large mixing bowl. Mash bananas with a fork until they are very mushy.
3. Add sugar, butter, vanilla and eggs. Mix on medium or high speed with an electric mixer until creamy. Use a rubber spatula to scrape sides of bowl if necessary.
4. Add baking powder, salt and baking soda and mix again with electric mixer. Add 1 cup of flour and mix again. Mix in remaining flour.
5. Drop 12 heaping teaspoons of the cookie dough on a cookie sheet approximately 2 inches apart. Place cookie sheet in preheated oven and bake approximately 12 to 15 minutes or until cookies are lightly browned.
6. When done, remove cookies with a metal spatula and place on a wire rack or a cut open brown paper bag to cool. Store in airtight container.

This recipe makes approximately 3 dozen cookies.

To make **"PUMPKIN COOKIES,"** *substitute 1 cup of solid packed pumpkin and 1 teaspoon cinnamon for the bananas.*

HOLIDAY COOKIES

1 cup butter
1½ cups sugar
3 eggs
2 teaspoons baking powder
7 Tablespoons milk
1 teaspoon baking soda
1 teaspoon salt
1 teaspoon vanilla extract
4½ cups flour

1. Let butter soften to room temperature.
2. Place butter in large mixing bowl. Add sugar and eggs. Mix with an electric mixer on medium or high speed until creamy. Scrape sides of bowl with a rubber spatula if necessary.
3. Add baking powder, milk, baking soda, salt and vanilla. Mix again with electric mixer until well combined. Add flour and mix again until completely blended.
4. Preheat oven to 400 degrees.
5. Dust work surface with flour before rolling out dough. Roll half of dough out at a time with a rolling pin until it is about ¼ of an inch thick. Also dust the top of the rolling pin if the dough sticks.
6. Cut cookies out with cookie cutters. Place on cookie sheet and bake 10 to 12 minutes or until edges are light brown.
7. When done, remove cookies with a metal spatula and place on a wire rack or a cut open brown paper bag to cool. Store in airtight container.

The yield will depend on what size cookie cutters you are using.
*Use the **"FROSTING FOR COOKIES"** recipe if you want to frost these cookies.*

FROSTING FOR COOKIES

6 Tablespoons butter
2 tablespoons milk
1 teaspoon vanilla extract
3 cups powdered sugar

1. Let butter soften to room temperature in large mixing bowl.
2. Add milk, vanilla and powdered sugar.
3. Mix on low speed with an electric mixer until ingredients are combined. Blend on high speed until soft and creamy. Scrape sides of bowl with a rubber spatula if necessary.
4. Frost cookies and let them sit out until frosting has hardened. Store in airtight container.

This recipe makes enough frosting to frost a batch of **"HOLIDAY COOKIES."**

Add food coloring to this frosting if you want colored frosting.

PEANUT BUTTER COOKIES

1 cup butter
1 cup peanut butter
1 cup granulated sugar
1 cup brown sugar, packed
2 eggs
½ teaspoon salt
½ teaspoon baking soda
2½ cups flour

1. Let butter soften to the room temperature.
2. Preheat oven to 350 degrees.
3. Place butter in large mixing bowl. Add peanut butter, sugars and eggs. Mix on medium or high speed with an electric mixer until creamy. Use a rubber spatula to scrape sides of bowl if necessary.
4. Add salt and baking soda to mixture and mix again with an electric mixer. Add 1 cup flour and mix again. Add remaining flour and mix again. If batter gets a bit too stiff for electric mixer, you may have to finish mixing with a spoon. When completely mixed, dough will be stiff and you will be able to form the dough into balls in your hand.
5. Roll a small amount of dough in the palm of your hands to make a 1-to 1½-inch dough ball. Place all dough balls onto a plate as you make them. There should be about 5 dozen.
6. Place 12 dough balls approximately 3 inches apart on a cookie sheet. Place cookie sheet in preheated oven and bake approximately 10 to 15 minutes or until cookies are light to medium brown.

7. When done, remove cookies with a metal spatula and place on a wire rack or a cut open brown paper bag to cool. Store in airtight container.

This recipe makes approximately 5 dozen cookies.

This recipe can also be made into a pan of bars. Press dough into 13-by-9-inch pan and bake approximately 20 minutes or until lightly browned.

HOT COCOA

---

2 cups instant nonfat dry milk
2 Tablespoons unsweetened cocoa powder
5 Tablespoons sugar

1. Put instant nonfat dry milk in medium mixing bowl. Add cocoa and sugar. Mix these dry ingredients with a fork until well combined.
2. Measure 1/3 cup of the instant cocoa mix and put it in a sandwich bag. Tie shut with a twist tie. This will make enough for 7 sandwich bags.
3. When you are ready to have some hot cocoa, pour contents of 1 sandwich bag into a mug. Boil ¾ cup water, then pour water into mug. Stir until well combined and serve.

This recipe makes 7 servings.

BROWNIES

1 cup butter
¾ cup granulated sugar
¾ cup brown sugar, packed
1 teaspoon vanilla extract
2 eggs
1 teaspoon baking soda
½ teaspoon salt
1/3 cup unsweetened cocoa powder
2¼ cups flour

1. Let butter soften to room temperature.
2. Preheat oven to 350 degrees.
3. In large mixing bowl, cream butter, sugars, vanilla and eggs with an electric mixer on medium speed until completely combined.
4. Add baking soda, salt and cocoa. Mix again with electric mixer on medium speed until completely combined and creamy. Scrape sides of bowl with a rubber spatula if necessary.
5. Add 1 cup of flour and mix again on medium speed until well combined. Add remaining flour and mix again. Scrape sides of bowl with a rubber spatula if necessary.
6. Grease a 13-by-9-inch pan. Pour batter into pan and spread it evenly across pan.
7. Bake in preheated oven approximately 20 minutes or until a knife inserted into center comes out clean. When they are done, remove brownies from oven and set pan on top of stove or on a wire rack to cool.

When the brownies have cooled, cut into 24 bars.

You can also make this recipe into approximately 3 dozen chocolate cookies by dropping heaping teaspoons of the dough on a cookie sheet approximately 2 inches apart. Bake 12 cookies at a time for 10 to 12 minutes or until done.

CHOCOLATE FROSTING

4 Tablespoons butter
2 cups powdered sugar
½ cup unsweetened cocoa powder
1 teaspoon vanilla extract
4 Tablespoons milk

1. Let butter soften to room temperature .
2. In medium or large mixing bowl, mix powdered sugar and cocoa with a fork until well combined.
3. Add butter, vanilla and milk. Mix with an electric mixer on medium speed until all ingredients are well combined and frosting is smooth. Scrape sides of bowl with a rubber spatula if necessary.
4. If frosting seems too stiff, add a little extra milk. If frosting seems too soft, add extra powdered sugar.

This will make enough frosting for a
13-by-9-inch cake or a batch of cupcakes.

*To make **"VANILLA FROSTING,"** eliminate the cocoa and decrease the milk by 1 Tablespoon.*

CHOCOLATE CAKE

3 cups flour
2 cups sugar
6 Tablespoons unsweetened cocoa powder
1 teaspoon salt
2 teaspoons baking soda
½ cup oil
2 Tablespoons vinegar
2 teaspoons vanilla extract
2 cups cold water

1. Preheat oven to 350 degrees.
2. Place flour in large mixing bowl. Add sugar, cocoa, salt and baking soda. Mix these dry ingredients with a fork until well combined.
3. Add oil, vinegar, vanilla and water. Mix with an electric mixer on medium speed until all ingredients are well combined and batter is smooth. Scrape sides of bowl with a rubber spatula if necessary.
4. Grease a 13-by-9-inch pan. Pour batter into pan.
5. Bake in preheated oven approximately 35 minutes or until a knife inserted into center comes out clean.
6. When cake is done, remove it from oven and set pan on top of the stove or on a wire rack to cool.
7. Frost cake when it has cooled.

This recipe makes 24 pieces.

You also can divide the batter between two 8-or 9-inch cake pans and make a double layer cake. Bake the cakes approximately 30 minutes or until done. You can also make this recipe into 42 cupcakes. Pour 1/8 cup of the batter into paper baking cups and bake for approximately 20 minutes or until a toothpick inserted into center comes out clean.

VANILLA CAKE

2 cups flour
1½ cups sugar
3 teaspoons baking powder
1 teaspoon salt
¾ cup oil
1 teaspoon pure vanilla extract
2 eggs
1 cup milk

1. Preheat oven to 350 degrees.
2. In large mixing bowl, combine flour, sugar, baking powder and salt. Mix these dry ingredients with a fork until well combined.
3. Add oil, vanilla, eggs and milk. Mix with an electric mixer on medium speed until all ingredients are well combined and batter is smooth. Scrape sides of bowl with a rubber spatula if necessary.
4. Grease 13-by-9-inch pan. Pour batter into pan.
5. Bake in preheated oven approximately 25 to 30 minutes or until a knife inserted into center comes out clean.
6. When cake is done, remove it from oven and set pan on top of stove or on a wire rack to cool.
7. Frost cake when it has cooled.

This recipe makes 24 pieces.
You also can divide the batter between two 8- or 9-inch cake pans and make a double layer cake. Bake the cakes approximately 25 to 30 minutes or until done. You can also make this recipe into approximately 30 cupcakes. Pour 1/8 cup batter into paper baking cups and bake approximately 20 to 25 minutes or until a toothpick inserted into center comes out clean.

PEANUT BUTTER CAKE

½ cup peanut butter
1/3 cup oil
1½ cups brown sugar, packed
2 eggs
2 cups flour
2 teaspoons baking powder
½ teaspoon ground cinnamon
½ teaspoon salt
1 cup milk

CRUMB TOPPING
2 Tablespoons butter
½ cup brown sugar, packed
½ cup flour
¼ cup peanut butter
½ teaspoon ground cinnamon

1. Preheat oven to 350 degrees.
2. Put peanut butter in large mixing bowl. Add oil, brown sugar and eggs. Mix with an electric mixer until well combined.
3. Add flour, baking powder, cinnamon, salt and milk. Mix again with an electric mixer on medium speed until well combined. Scrape sides of bowl with a rubber spatula if necessary.
4. Grease 13-by-9-inch pan. Pour batter into pan and spread it evenly around.
5. Prepare CRUMB TOPPING by melting butter in small saucepan over medium heat. Pour into medium mixing bowl. Add brown sugar, flour, peanut butter and cinnamon. Mash all ingredients with a fork or pastry cutter

until well mixed and crumbly. Sprinkle topping evenly over cake.

6. Bake in preheated oven approximately 25 to 30 minutes or until cake has browned and a knife inserted into center comes out clean.

7. When cake is done, remove it from oven and set pan on top of stove or on a wire rack to cool.

This recipe makes 24 pieces.

You can also make this recipe into 24 cupcakes. Divide batter and crumb topping among paper baking cups and bake approximately 20 minutes or until done.

RHUBARB CAKE

1½ cups sugar
½ cup oil
1 egg
2 cups flour
½ teaspoon salt
1 teaspoon baking soda
1 teaspoon vanilla extract
1 cup milk
3 cups chopped rhubarb
Topping:
¼ cup sugar
½ teaspoon ground cinnamon

1. Preheat oven to 350 degrees.
2. In large mixing bowl, combine sugar, oil and egg. Mix with an electric mixer until well combined. Scrape sides of bowl with a rubber spatula if necessary.
3. Add flour, salt, baking soda, vanilla and milk. Mix with electric mixer until well combined. Scrape sides of bowl with a rubber spatula if necessary.
4. Stir in chopped rhubarb.
5. Grease 13-by-9-inch pan. Pour batter into pan and spread it evenly around.
6. Prepare topping by mixing sugar and cinnamon together. Sprinkle topping evenly over cake.
7. Bake in preheated oven approximately 30 to 45 minutes or until cake has browned and a knife inserted into center comes out clean.
8. When cake is done, remove it from oven and set pan on top of stove or on a wire rack to cool.

This recipe makes 24 pieces.

*To make **"APPLE CAKE,"** substitute 3 cups of chopped apples for the chopped rhubarb in this recipe.*

9-INCH DOUBLE PIE CRUST

---

2 cups flour
1 teaspoon salt
½ cup butter
½ cup cold water

1. Let butter soften to room temperature.
2. Put flour and salt in large mixing bowl. Mix briefly with a fork to combine these dry ingredients.
3. Add butter. Cut butter into mixture with a fork or pastry cutter until butter is size of peas.
4. Pour in water and mix until a dough ball is formed. You may need to use your hands to knead a bit. Divide dough ball in half.
5. Dust work surface with flour before rolling out dough. Roll out one of the dough balls with a rolling pin to fit bottom of 9-inch pie pan. Also dust top of rolling pin if dough sticks. Roll out other dough ball for top crust.

This recipe makes one 9-inch double pie crust.

*Divide the recipe in half if only a bottom pie crust is necessary, i.e., **"PUMPKIN PIE."***

APPLE PIE

9-INCH DOUBLE PIE CRUST (see recipe on page 119)
6 cups peeled and chopped apples
1 cup sugar
1 teaspoon ground cinnamon

1. Prepare a **"9-INCH DOUBLE PIE CRUST."**
2. Preheat oven to 425 degrees.
3. Place apples in unbaked pie crust inserted into 9-inch pie pan.
4. In bowl, combine sugar and cinnamon with a fork. Sprinkle mixture over apples. Add top pie crust and pinch bottom crust and top crust together with a fork around edge of pan.
5. Poke approximately 6 vents in top of pie crust with a knife to let steam escape. Place a piece of aluminum foil on oven rack on which you will be placing pie, to catch any overflow. Place pie in preheated oven. Bake 10 to 15 minutes. Reduce heat to 350 degrees and bake additional 30 minutes or until pie is golden brown.
6. When pie is done, remove it from oven and let it cool on top of stove or on a wire rack.

This recipe makes 8 pieces.

PUMPKIN PIE

9-INCH DOUBLE PIE CRUST (see recipe on page 119)
1 cup sugar
1 teaspoon salt
1 teaspoon ground cinnamon
2 eggs
1 can (15-ounce) of solid packed pumpkin
¾ cup milk

1. Prepare ½ of a **"9-INCH DOUBLE PIE CRUST."**
2. Preheat oven to 425 degrees.
3. In large mixing bowl, combine sugar, salt, cinnamon, eggs, pumpkin and milk. Mix together with an electric mixer until well combined. Scrape sides of bowl with a rubber spatula if necessary.
4. Pour mixture into unbaked pie crust inserted into 9-inch pie pan.
5. Place pie in preheated oven. Bake 10 minutes. Reduce heat to 350 degrees and bake additional 60 minutes or until pie is set and knife inserted into center comes out clean.
6. When pie is done, remove from oven and let it cool on top of stove or on a wire rack.

This recipe makes 8 pieces.

Note-Do not use Ener-G egg Replacer in this recipe.

APPLE BARS

Crust:
¾ cup butter
2 cups flour
1 cup brown sugar, packed
½ cup quick cooking rolled oats

Filling:
6 cups peeled and chopped apples
1 cup granulated sugar
1 cup water
1 teaspoon vanilla extract
½ teaspoon ground cinnamon
¼ cup flour

1. Preheat oven to 350 degrees.
2. Place butter in small saucepan. Melt over medium to low heat. Pour into large mixing bowl.
3. Add flour, brown sugar and rolled oats. Mix with a fork or a pastry cutter until completely combined and evenly mixed. Reserve 1 cup of mixture and set aside to sprinkle over top of bars later on.
4. Grease a 13-by-9-inch pan and press remaining mixture into pan.
5. Spread chopped apples over crust.
6. Place granulated sugar in small saucepan. Add water, vanilla, cinnamon and flour. Cook over medium-low heat until thick, stirring while cooking with a fork or whisk. Pour mixture evenly over apples.
7. Spread reserved 1 cup sugar-oat mixture on top.
8. Bake in preheated oven approximately 45 minutes. When they are done, remove bars from oven and set pan on top

of stove or on a wire rack to cool.

This recipe makes 24 pieces.

To make **"RHUBARB BARS,"** *substitute 6 cups of chopped rhubarb for the apples.*

INDEX

ORDERING
INFORMATION

To order additional copies of this book, please provide the following information:

Name, Address, City, State, Zip

and send $14.99 per book ordered in the form of a check or money order.

Mail orders to:

Mary Jane & Jeff Cardarelle-Hermans
410 W. Montclaire Avenue
Glendale, WI 53217

We are always looking for additional economical recipes. If you have any you would like to share with our family, we would love to hear from you.